MY GOD
MY GLORY

TO MY FATHER ON EARTH
HENRY MILNER-WHITE, KT, LL.D.

1854 – 1922

whose own great goodness taught me true,
from earliest days,

OF OUR FATHER IN HEAVEN

MY GOD
MY GLORY

*Aspirations, Acts, and Prayers
on the desire for God*

THE LEGACY
AND DEVOTED TRIBUTE
OF
ERIC MILNER-WHITE
DEAN OF YORK

TO THE
ONE HOLY CATHOLIC APOSTOLIC
CHURCH

TRIANGLE

First published 1954
Definitive edition 1967
This edition 1994

Triangle
SPCK
Holy Trinity Church
Marylebone Road
London NW1 4DU

British Library Cataloguing in Publication Data

A catalogue record for this book is available from the
British Library.

ISBN 0-281-04728-6

Printed and bound in Great Britain by
BPC Paperbacks Ltd
A member of
The British Printing Company Ltd

Contents

APOLOGIA
PRO HOC LIBELLO

If they do nothing more, these Devotions bear witness to the joy and peace of one life lived in the full Faith of the Creeds, Sacraments, and Scriptures. For they have not been "written", but have grown in many years out of many meditations, many needs, and one Desire. From this angle they all are personal.

Is it seemly, some would ask, to print such in their framer's lifetime?

He would answer, first, that his life is now drawing to its close; and if, by God's grace, they may be helpful to individual or Church, their selection and arrangement had best be his own responsibility. No one else indeed could ever attempt it. Nor can anyone reach the heart of others except he speak from his own.

Remember, prayers do not record achievements, only desires; and acknowledgement of debt to the God of love.

Secondly, it may assist some Christians better to *see* prayer than to hear it described in book or pulpit. So-called "vocal" prayer does not always receive the attention it merits in the numerous books *about* prayer. Yet it must bear the whole weight of liturgical and public devotion and of an immense world of private. Moreover precise boundaries between vocal and mental prayer cannot be drawn; the one melts into the other, both ways, at all times; and ought to. Many "vocal forms" are but mental prayer compressed and uttered in a definite, legible structure for the benefit of the wider family of God. *The Lord's Prayer* itself is this. On the other hand, no private vocal prayer is well prayed without the pauses and ponderings which call out the powers of mind and heart. Whatever some books may suggest, prayer cannot be scientifically tabulated or indexed; it is a communion between the whole man and his God; and all the thousand manners of this commerce are blessed.

Again, however personally these prayers were first employed, in their matter and phrases they are only a mosaic of those spoken long ago by the Bible or by victorious servants of Christ:—by the incomparable, inexhaustible Book of Life and by the living Communion of Saints. Thank God for both in this very naughty world. All that is most lovely and true and of the Spirit in human life do these two immortal fountains keep alive and sparkling,—under the heaven of God.

As to use, three words, 1. Please do not treat this as a book to be read through, but as prayers to be prayed one at a time, on the due occasion. 2. The first person singular need only be turned into the plural, or into the third person, to change the form of many into direct intercession: e.g. *Deus Sacerdos* in the third person becomes at Embertide a supplication for Ordination candidates. 3. But their best employment is as a mere starting-point for the individual's own devotions, matches to light the experience which the Psalmist described once for all, *While I mused, the fire kindled and I prayed.*

Publisher's Note

Eric Milner-White's text from the definitive edition of 1967 is given in full here, the only changes and additional material being in the preliminary matter.

The Friends of York Minster, to whom the author gave the copyright to this book and who are receiving all royalties, have asked us to draw attention to the final paragraph of his Apologia (page xiv). Eric Milner-White encouraged users of the book to adapt the prayers to their own needs. The language can easily be modernised, as can be seen in this version of the prayer 'Coram Christo', which has been updated by the Right Reverend David Silk (Bishop of Ballarat, formerly Archdeacon of Leicester) and published in *In Penitence and Faith* (Mowbray/Cassell 1988).

Lord Jesus, let me condemn my sin in your company,
Face to face with your holiness.

Though I bow my head and heart in shame,
still let your hand clasp mine;
  let it be your love which searches me,
your sorrow which wakens my sorrow;
  and deepens it knowing
  I have wounded my Friend, my Master, my God.

Yea, Lord, I have crucified
  and crucify you again,
by many different sins,
  by often repeating each,
  by obeying, crowning, my self,

Forgive me, forgive me, Lord Jesus:
  Lord Jesus, wash me clean,
  Lord Jesus, make me whole,
  Lord Jesus, hold me fast
  In your company for ever.

The Life of
Eric Milner-White

Born in 1884, Eric Milner-White was educated at Harrow and King's College, Cambridge, where he achieved academic distinction. Trained for the ministry at Cuddesdon College, he served two curacies, and then returned to Cambridge as Chaplain of King's and Lecturer in History at Corpus Christi College. From 1914 he was Chaplain to the Forces (Senior Chaplain to the Seventh Division in 1917), was mentioned in despatches and awarded the DSO for conspicuous bravery in France. From 1918 to 1941 he was Dean and Fellow of King's. A Canon of Lincoln also from 1937, he was appointed Dean of York in 1941. He died in office in 1963.

His time at York was notable for his adornment of the Minster, the return of the medieval glass (removed during the war), and the exercise of liturgical skills in the ordering of services. In the City of York he was among the founders of the Civic Trust and the University. He was also Chairman of the Diocesan Advisory Committee, to which he brought his considerable artistic knowledge and judgement. For some years he was President of the Henry Bradshaw Society, was an Honorary Member of the Glaziers Company, and served on the Advisory Council of the Victoria and Albert Museum. He was awarded the CBE and honorary doctorates. An authority on, and collector of, modern pottery, he also purchased pictures, including those of Whistler, Sickert and Steer.

A champion of liturgical reform, he insisted on the dignity of language. Steeped as he was in the writings of classical Anglican divines, it is significant that the Prologue to this book of aspirations, acts and prayers is from the works of John Donne. This, one of his later compilations, is in the language of traditional spirituality, finely wrought, yet essentially simple.

Robert Holtby

Three books about Eric Milner-White have been published, of which only the most recent is still in print:

Patrick Wilkinson, *Eric Milner-White 1884–1963 — A Memoir* (King's College, Cambridge 1963);
Philip Pare and Donald Harris, *Eric Milner-White 1884–1963 — A Memoir* (SPCK 1965);
Robert Tinsley Holtby, *Eric Milner-White — A Memorial* (Friends of York Minster 1991).

Introduction

When I prepare to pray, I turn to *My God, My Glory*, and often, as a new day dawns, I turn to *My God, My Glory*. Indeed, this book of prayers has become so integral to my own prayer life that, several years ago, I wrote to the publisher, SPCK, requesting that it should be re-issued so that its gems could be made available to today's praying people. At that time a reprint was not feasible, but I continued to adapt the prayers for my own use. Then, quite out of the blue, as it were, I was informed that the way was now clear; the book was to be re-published. I count it a real privilege to have been invited to contribute this introduction.

I first stumbled on Dean Milner-White's prayers some twelve years ago. It was Advent and I was on retreat at the time. I still remember the sensation which swept over me as I pondered the first few lines of his Advent prayer:

O Lord, my years grow long,
  my time short:
Let me make haste with my repentance
  and bow head and heart:
Let me not stay one day from amendment,
  lest I stay too long . . .[1]

That phrase 'bow head and heart' touched me. At that time, I knew nothing about Eric Milner-White, yet, instinctively, I sensed that the person who had penned this prayer was one who enjoyed a rare and transparent intimacy with God. As I read on, I felt, increasingly, as though I was on hushed and holy ground – that I was not so much reading a prayer someone had written as praying with someone who was communing with God, and that that 'someone' was a man whose dearest desire was to draw ever closer to his Maker. By the time I reached the prayer's crescendo, my heart, too, was praying:

> Let me sing the new song,
>> following the Lamb whithersoever he goeth,
>> loving wheresoever he loveth,
>> doing whatsoever he biddeth,
>>> unto the perfect day
>>> and for ever and ever.[2]

The language, archaic though it appears when seen in print, posed no problems for me. I found myself automatically adapting and updating it as I echoed the yearnings which were being expressed:

> Let me sing the new song
>> following the Lamb wherever he goes,
>> loving whatever he loves,
>> doing whatever he asks,
>>> right up to the perfect day
>>> and beyond . . .
>>>> for ever and ever.[3]

For years, I attempted to discover who had breathed the prayers which were inspiring my own prayer. I longed to know what lay behind these carefully manicured meditations where not one word is wasted and where every word has been chosen with such care.

Eventually, I found that this cleric with whom I felt such a kinship had been Dean of York Minster, a member of the Church of England's Liturgical Commission and a member of the literary panel of the translators of the New English Bible. I read, with fascination, of the way he had pored over the Greek of the New Testament in an attempt to absorb its meaning before selecting for the New English Bible just the right word to capture the innuendoes of the text. I learned, with equal fascination, that his prayers as they appear in *My God, My Glory* are his polished versions of the original prayers of his heart; that, in his manuscript book, the original prayer was rearranged and reordered many times with meticulous care, many crossings out and substitutions. And I was touched to read that many of these meditations had been born during wakeful night hours when the Dean, an insomniac, would turn his sleeplessness into prayerfulness. Most moving of all, I unearthed this testimony from the book, *Eric Milner-White: A Memoir*:

Milner-White was more than a compiler of prayers. He was concerned to lead others in the spirit of prayer, and in that way of contemplation which is nearer to daily life than many people realise.[4]

Although the Dean had died before I met his book, I realised that his main ministry lives on. Through *My God, My Glory* he continues to 'lead others into the spirit of prayer'. Through the distillation of his own meditations and through his own expressed heart-longing for God, he continues to woo readers from deep to deep. This prompts me to reiterate, from the richness of personal experience, the acclaim of his biographers:

Only a man of prayer, of simplicity and sincerity, could write such a book, and it will bring great help to those who will use it in the spirit in which it is written. It is a book which brings contemplation near to the circumstances of every day.[5]

It is my personal prayer that this re-issue of these meditative pieces may nurture the prayer of individuals, groups and entire congregations in the way they have fed me; that many may capture the Dean's wonder on waking:

Lord, let me find you in all things to-day . . .
Your light touches creation all around
    with a brightness from heaven:
in the light of your joy our hearts leap;
    in the light of your love our eyes see;
in the light of the glory of your grace
    let me learn and love, do well and be glad.

For this environment of the divine,
    this peep into glory,
    for the new births of a new day,
let me be glad and rejoice, let me give thanks,
    O my Endless, Only Day,
    to-day, all day, always.[6]

That, at night, many may pray:

Look down this night, O Lord God, with compassion
    on all who dread its approach;

who suffer and can find no sleep.
Through the long watches grant them
    awareness of your Presence,
    support and solace from your love . . .

O Lord God, let the night soon pass,
    and the day break bright with your healing,
        your peace.[7]

And that, during the hours sandwiched between waking and sleeping, in times of need and in times of joy, on 'ordinary' days and on Feast Days, many will tune into the love of the ever-present Christ through the medium of this evergreen book.

Joyce Huggett
Cyprus, 1994

Notes

1 Eric Milner-White, *My God, My Glory*, p. 12.
2 *ibid*., p. 12.
3 My adaptation of the Advent prayer.
4 Philip Pare and Donald Harris, *Eric Milner-White 1884-1963 — A Memoir*, (SPCK 1965), p. 105.
5 *ibid*., p. 106.
6 *My God, My Glory*, p. 13.
7 *ibid*., p. 22.

Prologue

*by the Very Reverend John Donne D.D.
Dean of St Paul's (1621 — 1631)*

God gave me the light of nature, when I quickened in my mother's womb by receiving a reasonable soul: and God gave me the light of faith when I quickened in my second mother's womb, the church, by receiving my baptism; but in my third day, when my mortality shall put on immortality, he shall give me the light of glory, by which I shall see himself. To this light of glory, the light of honour is but a glow-worm; amd majesty itself is but a twilight; the cherubims and seraphims are but candles; and that Gospel itself, which the apostle calls the glorious Gospel, but a star of the least magnitude . . . St Augustine sums it up fully upon those words, *In lumine tuo, In thy light we shall see light, te scilicet in te,* we shall see thee in thee; that is, says he, *face to face.*

Sermon xxi

Our voyage lies about the hemisphere of glory, for, *All the upright in heart shall glory.* So no man shall come to the glory of heaven, that hath not a holy ambition of this glory in this world; for the glory of God shines through godly men.

Sermon lxvii

Almighty God made us for his glory, and his glory is in our happiness.

Sermon cxvi

I
PRAYERS BEFORE PRAYER

THE HID TREASURE

IN THE FIELD of my soul
    there is a treasure hidden.
O my soul, dost thou not know?
    hast thou no desire for it, art thou seeking?

No human eye can detect it, nor hand handle;
    secret and silent it lies,
        too deep to reach or reckon.
Yet it is THERE, and it is mine:
I have not bought it, nor inherited,
    still less deserved;
        it is Gift.
By Spirit alone can I awake to it,
    by faith alone find,
        only by love possess.

So wake, spirit of mine, to the search!
    Be my faith resolute to find,
        my love strong to hold!
And then, in the field of my soul,
    THOU art there,
        THOU, my Lord and my God:
more bright than light itself,
    over me like a banner,
    under me, a strong rock,
    around me as a house of defence,
    before me, a beckoning star;
but, richest of all, WITHIN,
        my Treasure for ever:
hidden still, yet Life of my life to-day;
    to-morrow, my open Glory
        my LORD, my GOD.

BEFORE PRAYER

I

LORD, who givest the will to pray,
    make my prayer good,
humble, ardent, and effectual,
    by the kindling of thy Spirit;
    by the sincerity of my soul,
        its conformity to thy will,
            its order to thy glory;
    by the devotion of my heart,
        the strong tranquillity of its faith,
        the wide charity of its desires,
        the fervour of its love,
            and the importunity of its pleading;
    through Jesus Christ our Lord.

II

LORD, thou hast given me this space for prayer:
    fill it with thy gifts of grace;
    fill it with the shewings of thy truth,
            with holy counsels and inspirations,
            with the communion of peace;

Occupy it with the work of love—
                to beg thy mercies upon them I love,
                upon all mine acquaintance,
                upon all in need,
                upon all whom thou lovest.

Overshadow me with thy Spirit,
                with the light that is THOU;
Banish distraction, inattention, coldness;
Make mine eyes to see, mine ears to hear,
                my tongue to speak, my soul to be still;
And then be merciful to my prayer,
                and to me, a sinner;
                        for Christ's sake.

4

RENEWAL

LORD GOD, that art the First and the Last,
    grant me a new beginning—
        a new desire to pray
        and new resolution in setting apart the hours
            for speech with thee:
        new ambition in prayer
            that it may be humbler, quieter, void of self,
             all to thy glory:
        new vision of the Light,
            which is beyond brightness, and above joy:
        new listening for thy counsel and command,
            acceptance of thy will,
            fervour to obey it,
            patience and strength to suffer for it:
        new union and communion with thy Holy Spirit,
            that I pray his mind
             and he my prayer.

O Lord, who on the throne of thrones
        makest all things new,
      renew my prayer;
          renew me in thyself
            and hold me there.

WORK OF PRAYER

MY GOD and Father,
    help me to pray
        as my first work,
        mine unremitting work,
        my highest, finest, and dearest work:
    as the work I do for thee, and by thee,
        and with thee,
        for other thy children and for the whole world.

Infuse and influence it with thy blessed Spirit,
    that it be not unwilling, nor unworthy, nor in vain;
    that it be not occupied with my own concerns,
        nor dwell in the interests dear to myself,
        but seek thy purposes, thy glory only;
    that it be holy and more holy unto the Holiest,
        and ever and all through thy Son,
        my Saviour Jesus Christ.

PRAY IN THE SPIRIT

O HOLY SPIRIT OF GOD,
    which are the moments I never regret?
These, which the days and years have certified,
    the moments spent in prayer:
too few, inattentive, stuffed with self,
    grudged often, often refused:
yet source of thine unstinted aid,
        wells of contrition, founts of joy;
     crying in thy close company, by thine own breath,
        Abba, Father.

Yet still and ever, O most Holy,
    I know not what to pray for as I ought.
Teach me to pray. Help me to pray WITH THEE,
    who searchest out the deep things of God.
Bring my prayer into such true accord
        with thy good will and pleasure,
that thou canst make it thine own,
    with pleading too urgent for utterance,
        or for denial.

Abba, Father. Carry my small prayers,
        O merciful Spirit,
    folded in grace so intimate,
    lifted by might so strong,
        up to the heavenlies.
Carry my right desires into Jesus' intercession;
carry my whole soul's longing into the Father's heart,
        now, always.

BEFORE SERVICE IN CHURCH

LET me come into the church of God
    to meet the Spirit of God:
  not to give religion an hour,
    but to live in the eternal;
  not to maintain a decorous habit,
    but to bow in the holy place before the Holy
      One;
  not to judge the words of a preacher,
    but to draw life from the Word and Truth
      everlasting;
  not to be moved or soothed by music,
    but to sing from the heart divine praises;
  not that mine eyes roam over architecture or
      congregation,
    but that my soul look up to the King in his
      beauty,
    and my heart plead the needs of his children;
  not that my thoughts escape out into the world,
    but that they be still, and know that thou art
      GOD.

Let me go, and go again, into the house of the Lord,
    and be glad, and give thanks, and adore
      my King and my GOD.

POSTULATIONES PRO OMNIBUS

LORD, when I pray, and petition thee for thy grace,
hear not that prayer as intended or made for my single self:
    but always for others, with like desire or need:
    for all for whom I would or ought to pray,
    for my family and companions' sakes,
    for those whom I shall meet, to-day, to-morrow:

    for all others of thy family, thy Church,
        thy mystical Body, full with needs;
    for the departed that live unto thee,
        the living that die unto themselves,
    for them that have forsaken thy grace,
        or never have known it.

O Saviour of the world, in need we all are one,
        needing thee:
    let all be in my every prayer,
    so that each be spoken with a thousand voices
        for a thousand wants,
    and come into that heavenly intercession,
    which thou dost offer with thy wounds.
Yea, let it be spoken with a thousand thousand voices
    by angels, archangels and the company of heaven,
    with the persistence of my whole heart,
    and with the pleading of the Spirit himself,
        before the Father's throne.

BEFORE MEDITATION

I

LORD, send thy Holy Spirit into my soul
    to tranquillize and to stir,
    to draw and to drive,
    to enlighten and to inflame,
as I study the Word;
    and thy covenant in thy Word;
    and thy grace in thy covenant;
    and thy goodness in thy grace;
    and thy glory in thy goodness;
and THYSELF in thy glory,
    the Almighty, the Eternal,
    the Lover and Perfecter of souls,
    the Father, the Son, and the Holy Ghost,
      one God, for ever and ever.

II

SPEAK, Lord for thy servant heareth.
    My knees are bowed, mine eyes close,
      I cover my face, I forget the earth.

O Lord, my heart is ready, my heart is ready;
    my mind awake, attent, alert;
    my spirit open and ardent,
      abandoning all else,
      holding itself in leash,
      straining the eye of faith,
      hearkening for thy step, distant and nearer,
      leaping with love,
      throbbing loudly, yet lying still;

Speak, Lord, for thy servant heareth.

SECRET TABERNACLE

LORD, grant me only this grace—
    when my time is my own,
    when my time is not my own,
        yet always to commune with thee:
    through all the concerns of earth
        let my conversation be in heaven.

Lord, let me speak with thee
        in the secret place of thy tabernacle:
    let me hear the still, small voice
        of thine eternal WORD:
    impart to me the testimonies
        of eternal Truth;
    encompass me
        with thy eternal Spirit.

Give me the joy of work that endures
        by learning and doing thy will;
    shew me the glories that last;
    grant me abiding peace
        in the light of thy countenance.

Lord, let me love the habitation of thy house,
        and dwell in it all the days of my life:
let me offer there mine oblation of great gladness,
        and sing and speak praises unto my God,
          now and for ever.

ADORATION OF A SON

O MY FATHER,
  I thank thee, I praise thee,
  that by thy love thou hast led me
    and called me,
    humbled and pardoned me,
    recalled me, repardoned me,
    roused and rearmed me
      against myself and against the world.

O my GOD,
  I believe and I hope in thee,
  that by thy love thou wilt bring me
    nearer to thyself by some faithfulnesses,
    nearer by my many failures,
    nearer by joy and nearer by pain,
    nearest by loving others in thee
      to the end.

Yea, I adore and will love thee,
    until thou wholly possess
    and frame and fulfil me
  like unto Christ, in Christ, all Christ's,
  a son in whom thou art well pleased,
    O my Father,
      my God.

II
TIME,
MORNING AND
EVENING

THE HALLOWING OF TIME

I

O MY GOD
    all times are thy times,
    and every day thy day,
    made lovely only with thy light.
Bring us, O Lord, to that blessed eternal day
    which thy Son our Saviour hath won for us,
    and to the perfect light.

II

Blessed be the hour, O Christ, in which thou wast born,
    and the hour in which thou didst die;
Blessed be the dawn of thy rising again,
    and the high day of thine ascending:
O most merciful and mighty Redeemer Christ,
    let all times be the time of our presence with thee,
    and of thy dwelling in us.

ADVENT

O LORD, my years grow long,
      my time short:
Let me make haste with my repentance
      and bow head and heart:
Let me not stay one day from amendment,
      lest I stay too long:
Let me cease without delay
      to love my own mischief,
and abandon without a backward look
      the unfruitful works of darkness.

Lord, grant me new watchfulness
      to lay hold upon opportunity of good:
Make me at last put on
      the whole armour of light:
Rank me among them who work for their Lord,
      loins girded, lamps burning,
         till the night shall pass
            and the true light shine.

Let me sing the new song,
      following the Lamb whithersoever he goeth,
      loving wheresoever he loveth,
      doing whatsoever he biddeth,
         unto the perfect day
            and for ever and ever.

ON WAKING

I

O LORD, when I awake, and day begins,
    waken me to thy Presence;
    waken me to thine indwelling;
    waken me to inward sight of thee,
        and speech with thee,
        and strength from thee;
    that all my earthly walk may waken into song
    and my spirit leap up to thee all day,
        all ways. Amen.

II

ANOTHER day of wonder
    thou givest, O Lord,
in which to learn, to love, to do well, and to be glad.
Lord, let me find thee in all things to-day;
    be thou my Endless Day.

Thy light touches creation all around
    with a brightness from heaven:
in the light of its joy our hearts leap;
    in the light of thy love our eyes see;
in the light of the glory of thy grace
    let me learn and love, do well and be glad.

For this environment of the divine,
    for this peep into glory,
    for the new births of a new day,
let me be glad and rejoice, let me give thanks,
    O my Endless, Only Day,
    to-day, all day, always.

EVERY DAY

O MY GOD,
   never is he alone that hath thee in his thought
         and thy will in his sight:
   nor ever are his undertakings vain,
      who calleth thee to their beginnings.

   So, Lord, give me desire and grace
            this day and every day
   to claim thy Presence and come reverently into it,
         to bow before thee,
         to partake of thee,
         to dwell in thee,
            all the day and every day:

   to grow and bear fruit from thee,
         to walk beside thee,
         to work for thee,
         to speak and listen to thee,
         to love with thee and by thy measure,
         to repose upon thee,
            all the day and every day;

   faithfully, humbly, tirelessly, passionately,
            this day and for ever.

TO-DAY

LORD, help us to add to the world's tale of goodness
to-day, in thy Name and by thine aid.

Lord, in all the love, joy, and loveliness about our path
this day, let us descry thine hand and praise thee.

Lord, in this day's difficulties, keep us serene of heart
and faithful to thy will.

Lord, do thou open opportunity this day to bear with
thee the pains and burdens of others.

Lord, grant us to-day to contend for truth, if only by
a word.

Lord, make our faith this day to grow and glow, as a
flame leaping upward.

Yea Lord, while it is called to-day, let thy countenance
lighten upon us
that we may advance from weakness to glory,
from struggle to peace,
towards the perfect day and the endless light. Amen.

CHOICE

LORD, in the choices of every day,
    grant me to choose aright
        as in thy Presence and to thy glory:
to discriminate not only between the good and the evil
    but between the good and the better,
        and to do the best.

Save me from treason to thee,
    O my Master and King,
    by disguising to myself thy demands,
    by any choice of ashes for bread,
    by any surrender to popular standards,
    by any accommodation of duty or faith
        to mine own ease,
    by any the least betrayal of purity.

Rather grant me the Spirit of judgment
    to choose with clear eyes
        the ways of grace,
    the eternal wisdom and the eternal will:
not only to choose, but to pursue
    all that is true, all that is of good report,
        all that is lovely;
and in all to exalt thy praise and honour,
        my LORD and my GOD.

DOMINUS EST

IT IS THE LORD!
In the morning, at noonday, in the night season
thou comest, dost await us, wouldst accompany and bless:
in street and sanctuary, office and home, at work, after
work,
alike in moments of dismay and happiness,
It is the Lord!

It is the Lord, lying on straw—
and the small things and the humble burn with holy
fire.
It is the Lord, kneeling in desert, on mountain,
in the garden,
beside us as we pray.
It is the Lord, without the gate, shewing his wounds,
to interpret and soothe our pain;
the Lord, risen and raising us
unto his likeness, his life, his crown.
O Lord, thou art amongst us;
open our eyes to see
and help our faith, scarcely believing for joy,
to take hold of thee;
now, as of old in the Upper Room, by the lakeside,
It is the Lord!

It is THOU; and in thee is all.
Though we be sinful men
depart not from us;
O Lord, leave us not, we beseech thee;
abide with us always.

THE VOICE

THERE came a Voice from heaven
    which everyone of the truth heareth;
the voice of a Child
    made man amongſt men;
the voice of a Son
    pleasing the Father;
the voice of the Sinless
    forgiving sin;
the voice of the Shepherd
    leading the flock;
the voice of a Saviour
    from a Cross;
voice from the Majeſty,
    BEHOLD I MAKE ALL THINGS NEW.

Lo! the living God doth send out his voice,
    yea, and that a mighty voice—
The Lord, even the moſt mighty God, hath spoken,
    calling the world,
    calling, recalling, me,

SEEK YE MY FACE.
    Thy face, Lord, will I seek.
WHOM SHALL I SEND AND WHO WILL GO FOR US?
    Lord, send me.

WORK

O LORD GOD, in this our world of industry,
    make us to be more generous and joyful
        in our daily work;
    that each may propose for himself and perform,
        the utmost he would expect from others.

Keep us from dissipating time,
    from betraying those who remunerate us,
    from shirking the less pleasant,
    from sloth of hand or mind
        which worketh death.

O Lord, who rewardest every man according to his work,
    grant us the spirit of honesty and thoroughness;
        a passion for good craftsmanship;
        the inspiration of giving,
           of giving the best,
           of giving yet more,
           and not ceasing to give.

So bless our work; thou canst not bless idleness:
bless it that we may love that for which we labour,
    performing it as to thee and not to men,
    intending simply and faithfully thy glory;
    offering ourselves in our labours
    and dedicating their products
        and pleasures and pains alike to thee,
           while it is yet day:
for the night cometh when no man can work.

EVENING PRAYER

LORD, the day which thou hast given is over;
  yet the light of my gratitude this day
    for all the powers and joys of thy providing,
    and for the kindlinesses of men, does not fail:
  thou hast been very merciful, O my GOD.

But draw the darkness deep
  over my lost opportunities and failures,
  the ungenerous thought, the word ill spoken, the
    deed ill done,
  all hurt of others and indulgence of myself:
be merciful, be very merciful, O my GOD.

Be merciful: guard my unconscious hours;
  for thou, Lord, it is who givest sleep
    to crown thy daily gifts;
  thou, who dost transform darkness into blessing
  with rest to the body, peace to the mind:
    thanks be to thee, O my GOD.

Yet let my soul, freed from the prisons of day,
  turn to the prayer of trust,
  mount on wings of faith
  and chant canticles of praises
    at the windows of heaven;
  where is no night, where thou art listening always,
    O my most merciful GOD.

NUNC DIMITTIS

THE DAY fails; the darkness falls.
  Now, O Lord my GOD,
  now let thy servant lay him down in peace;
      for it is thou, Lord, only
          that makeſt him dwell in safety.

Out of mine own night let me call, let me cry,
    that I sleep not in sin unrepented.
Let my hands be clean,
      let my prayer be pure;
      let me look up to the brightness of thy glory,
        with whom is no darkness at all.
Let my lying down be very truſt,
      mine eyes close under thy blessing.
Let action sleep, and memory, and even thought;
      but not love, never my hope in thee.
Into thy hands, O Lord,
      I commend my spirit.

While the body reſts,
      quiet in thy keeping,
    let my soul ascend
      and sing in thy light:
Hosanna in the higheſt.

FOR THE SLEEPLESS

LOOK DOWN this night, O Lord God, in pity
    on all who dread its approach;
    who suffer and can find no sleep.
Through the long watches grant them
    awareness of thy Presence,
    support and solace from thy love.

Comfort, O comfort them, dearest Lord,
    who thyself drank the bitter cup
        deeper than us all;
    drank, full with agony,
        but empty of complaint;
    then, *for* us;
        now, ever, *with* us.

By thy Passion grant them power of patience,
    and a new true fellowship of surprise and joy
        with One Crucified, their God;
so that they be well content to offer him
        their prayer and pain and courage;
and to spend the slow hours with the choirs of heaven,
    singing from the heart their faith,
        Alleluia, Alleluia.

O Lord God, let the night soon pass,
    and the day break bright with thy healing,
        thy peace.

III
PENITENCE
AND DEPRECATION

LENT

LORD, bless to me this Lent.

Lord, let me fast most truly and profitably,
    by feeding in prayer on thy Spirit:
        reveal me to myself
            in the light of thy holiness.

Suffer me never to think
    that I have knowledge enough to need no teaching,
        wisdom enough to need no correction,
        talents enough to need no grace,
        goodness enough to need no progress,
        humility enough to need no repentance,
        devotion enough to need no quickening,
        strength sufficient without thy Spirit;
  lest, standing still, I fall back for evermore.

Shew me the desires that should be disciplined,
    and sloths to be slain.
Shew me the omissions to be made up
    and the habits to be mended.
And behind these, weaken, humble, and annihilate in me
    self-will, self-righteousness, self-satisfaction,
    self-sufficiency, self-assertion, vainglory.

May my whole effort be to return to thee;
    O make it serious and sincere
    persevering and fruitful in result,
        by the help of thy Holy Spirit
        and to thy glory,
            my Lord and my GOD.

REPENTANCE

LORD, when for joy I seek thy Presence,
       give me a godly sorrow for my sins;
       yea, and for my righteousnesses also.

O Lord that my sins may be covered,
       strengthen me to uncover them
              honestly, unsparingly,
              before thine infinite love.

Let my heart with all its secrets
       be thrown as open to thee
              as thy mercies to me.

May I never confess my faults
       with no purpose to leave them
       nor make half-repentances,
              lest I make none.

Rather let me lift up to thee
       all my prides and shames,
              the stubborn and the small,
              the recurrent and the continuous,
       that they may be buried low.
              and have no resurrection.

SELF-EXAMINATION

HELP me, O Holy Spirit, to search and question myself,
          and honestly to answer:
Am I single-minded in seeking my God?
          in serving him? even in praying to him?
Do I put GOD first in deed? in intention?
          or even in desire? in hope?
What reserves do I always maintain against him?
          what other loves cling to?
Is not self-regard my prevailing motive,
          secret, silent, undetectable, insatiable?
Where do I serve self in daily conduct,
          when I should be serving others?
          when I should be serving GOD?
Do I obey self even in the most inward spiritual things?
          in the exercise of holy ministries?
                    even in the holiest place?

Search me thyself, O GOD,
          seek the grounds of my heart;
Look well if there be any way of wickedness in me,
          any subservience to mine ease,
          any hungering and playing for mine own honour.
Help, O help me slay my self-regard,
          the foe that is in myself and of myself,
                    and to want to slay it.
O Saviour of the world,
     who by thy Cross and precious Blood hast redeemed us,
save me and help me,
          I humbly beseech thee, O Lord.

CORAM CHRISTO

LORD JESUS, let me condemn my sin
IN THY COMPANY,
FACE TO FACE WITH THY HOLINESS.

Though I bow my head and heart in shame,
    still let thy hand clasp mine;
  let it be thy love which searches me,
      thy sorrow which wakens my sorrow;
      and deepens it knowing
          I have wounded my Friend,
              my Master, my God.

Yea, Lord, I have crucified
      and crucify thee again,
      by many different sins,
      by often repeating each,
      by obeying, crowning, my self.
Forgive me, forgive me, Lord Jesus:
      Lord Jesus, wash me clean,
      Lord Jesus, make me whole,
      Lord Jesus, hold me fast
            IN THY COMPANY
            for ever.

CONFESSION

FORGIVE me, O Lord,
O Lord forgive me my sins,
    the sins of my youth,
    the sins of the present;
    the sins I laid upon myself in an ill pleasure,
    the sins I cast upon others in an ill example;
    the sins which are manifest to all the world,
    the sins which I have laboured to hide from mine
        acquaintance,
      from my own conscience,
      and even from my memory;

    my crying sins and my whispering sins,
    my ignorant sins and my wilful;
    sins against my superiors, equals, servants,
      against my lovers and benefactors,
    sins against myself, mine own body, my own soul;
    sins against thee, O almighty Father, O merciful Son,
      O blessed Spirit of GOD.

Forgive me, O Lord, forgive me all my sins;
Say to me, *Son be of good comfort*
      thy sins are forgiven thee
    in the merits of thine Anointed,
      my Saviour Jesus Christ.

A BRIEF GENERAL CONFESSION

ALMIGHTY GOD,
    long-suffering and of great goodness;
We confess to thee, we confess with our whole heart,
    our neglect and forgetfulness of thy commandments;
    our wrong doing, speaking, and thinking;
    the hurts we have done to others;
    and the good we have left undone.

O God, forgive thy people
    that have sinned against thee:
    and raise us to newness of life:
      through Jesus Christ our Lord.
                    Amen.

PROFESSING AND DOING

I

LORD, when thou hast bidden,
    I have said "I will";
            —and have not done it.
             Lord, forgive me.

LORD, when thou hast bidden,
    I have said "I will not".
            Lord forgive me,
    and make me better than my word,
          to do it,
            for thy dear sake.

II

LORD God Almighty,
    let not mine obedience be without devotion,
        nor my faith without fervour,
        nor my penitence without compunction,
        nor my prayer without intention of spirit and
           attention of mind:
    let not by meditation be without strengthening
          of holy desires,
        nor my communions without oblation,
        nor my good purposes without performance,
        nor my discourse and deeds without love,
        nor my love without sacrifice;
        for the sake of my Lord Jesus Christ.

A PARVULIS LIBERA ME, DOMINE

KEEP me, O Lord,
>from the little, the interfering, and the stupid;
from the infection of irritation and anger over nothings;
>*Deliver me, and keep me, O my Lord.*

from all promptings to decry the person or work of others;
from scorn, sarcasm, petty spite, and whisperings behind
>the back;
from the dishonest honesty of frankness meant to hurt;
>*Deliver me, and keep me, O my Lord.*

from hasty judgments, biased judgments, cruel judg-
>. ments, and all pleasure in them;
from resentment over disapproval or reproof, whether
>just or unjust;
>*Deliver me, and keep me, O my Lord.*

from all imposition of my own fads and interests
>upon my acquaintance;
from burdening and boring others with
>my own anxieties and ailments;
from self-justification, self-excusing, and complacency;
>*Deliver me, and keep me, O my Lord.*

DE VANITATIBUS

KEEP me, O Lord,
  from all things which come to nothing,
    out of which in thy kingdom nothing can
        proceed,
    or that count for less or worse than nothing
        upon earth;
            Keep me, good Lord.

From absorptions which bear no fruit,
    thoughts that are empty,
    and hasty compliances with evil;
  from phantasies and obsessions,
    and all baseness to my own soul;
        Keep me, good Lord.

From indolence and intolerance of mind;
    all impulses and schemes of vain glory;
  from self-complacency;
        Keep me, good Lord.

Let this be both my ambition and my peace:
    to walk in thy light,
        that I may become a son of light;
    to bring forth the fruits of the Spirit,
        that I may grow into thy likeness;
    and to abide in thy love
        who first lovedst me;
            who lovest to the end,
                without end.

AGAINST COMPLACENCY

O MY GOD,
> what have I that I have not received?
>> —received of thee?

Thou madest me out of nothing,
> and with untiring ease hast bestowed
>> and bestowest all things.

From thee cometh every good desire,
> every aptitude and talent,
> the acquisition of knowledge
>> and the employment of it;

from thy wisdom come warnings, disciplines, illuminations
>> along all the way;

from thy strength, armour;
from thy love, my faith, my calling, my work;
>> and the multitude of my joys;
>>> —thou givest all.

Therefore, O Lord, still by thy bounty,
> deliver me from human complacency,
> from manœuvrings for the praise of men,
> from self-glorying, open and veiled,
> from modesty falsely assumed,
> from absorption in my own interests,
> from the fevers of self-gratification.

Rather, O Lord, let me seek in all things thy glory,
> assisting in every good work
>> and forgetting my part in it;
> begetting fruits which, as they are thy gift
>> and thy will,
>>> shall be all to thy praise.

SELF-NOUGHTING

LORD, bestow on me two gifts,
    —to forget myself,
    —never to forget thee.

Keep me from self-love, self-pity, self-will,
    in every guise and disguise,
nor ever let me measure myself by myself.
Save me from Self,
    my tempter, seducer, jailer;
    corrupting desire at the spring,
    closing the avenues of grace,
    leading me down the streets of death.

Rather, let my soul devote to thee
    its aspirations, affections, resolutions;
let my mind look unto thee
    in all its searchings, strivings, certitudes;
let my body work for thee
    with its full health and abilities.

Let thy love pass
    into the depth of my heart,
    into the heart of my prayer,
    into the prayer of my whole being;
so that I desert myself
    and dwell and move in thee,
        in peace, now and evermore.

JESU, Creator,
>> Recreate and renew me.

Jesu, Saviour,
>> Save me from sin,
>> Save me from self.

Jesu, High Priest,
>> Pity me,
>> Plead for me,
>> Pardon and purify me.

Jesu, Prophet,
>> Waken and warn me.

Jesu, King,
>> Rule me.

Jesu, the Way,
Jesu, my friend,
>> Go with me always.

Jesu, the Truth,
>> Teach me, counsel me,
>> Make me all true.

Jesu, true Light,
>> Scatter my darkness.

Jesu, true Bread,
>> Strengthen my weakness.

Jesu, good Shepherd.
>> Lead me and feed me.

Jesu, the Life,
>> Live in me always,
>>> that I may adore thee,
>>> my Lord and my God,
>>>> evermore. Amen.

RELEASE

WHERE the Spirit of the Lord is, there is liberty.

ENTER my heart, O Holy Spirit,
 to break the bonds of sin;
 to bring one fallen out of his prisons
  of sinful habit and wrong desire,
  of indolence and self-will.
Come, O Holy Spirit, come in blesséd mercy,
  and set me free.

Throw open, O Lord, the locked gates of my mind;
 plant in its garden the seed of good graces
  and nurse them into flower;
 cleanse the chambers of my thought for thy dwelling;
 light there the fires of thine own holy brightness
  in new understandings of truth,
  new visions of GOD.
Come, O Holy Spirit, come in blesséd mercy,
  and set me free.

O Holy Spirit, unshackle my soul
 from every dungeon which shuts it in,
  and would shut thee out:
 give it the wings of the morning
  and the jubilation of the freed
  to fly to its home, its rest, its Lord.
Come, O Holy Spirit, come in thy blesséd mercy
  and set me free.

O Holy Spirit, very GOD, whose Presence is liberty,
 grant me the perfect freedom
  to be thy servant
 to-day, to-morrow, evermore.

DEBT

CAUSE me, O Lord my GOD,
    more and more to comprehend and acknowledge
        what I owe thee,
        what I owe others,
        what I owe myself.

I

The first, ten thousand thousand talents,
        I cannot pay.
O may thy merciful grace forgive the debt,
        and accept interest upon it,
            though it be but in farthings,
by praise for all I have received from thee,
        my being, well-being, and eternal hope:
by prayer for all thou desirest still to give,
        of daily grace and eternal glory:
by love for the love that ever loves me.
Let me pay thee the most that I may
        in the coin of faith and obedience
            which thine own Spirit minteth in me;
        and grow most out of debt
            by falling yet more deeply into it.

II

Let me render my dues
    and pay my debts to others:
        to the King, honour and loyalty;
        to pastors, masters, benefactors,
        and all servants of my happiness and health,
                gratitude;
        to them that love me, love;
        to my friends and acquaintances, integrity and
                trust;
        to all men, reverence and kindliness;
           for thou lovest and hast died for all.

III

And make me a good paymaster to mine own soul,
    rendering to thee a good account of my stewardship.
Suffer me never to put off repentance:
    make me wise and learned in the best art,
        of knowing thee;
    rich and mighty in the best treasure,
        of doing thy will.
Except thou build the house,
        I labour but in vain;
    except thou keep my city,
        it must fall.

CONVERSION

OLD THINGS are passed away:
    all things are become new.
GOD hath broken down the bars of the gates;
    there's no prison more, no fetters, no barriers.
One thing I know; whereas I was shut in, now am I free:
And another; whereas I was blind, now I see.
I KNOW THAT I HAVE PASSED FROM DEATH UNTO LIFE.

Whichever way I look,
    it is love that filleth all things,
        the love of God, God who is love.
I am astonished, I am free, I sing for joy.
I KNOW THAT I HAVE PASSED FROM DEATH UNTO LIFE.

No more am I enclosed in myself;
    no more feed on the imaginations of pride
        nor brood on the slights to it:
    gone are self-conscious terrors and timidities,
        gone the aimlessness and petty judgments.
I KNOW THAT I HAVE PASSED FROM DEATH UNTO LIFE.

Mine, suddenly, is fellowship with all men;
    mine, wonderfully, fellowship with GOD,
        who speaks, quickens, reveals, transforms;
    mine the company of the redeemed in Christ,
        who cry to their new-born brethren—
"Now are ye light in the Lord.
    walk as children of light.
    Arise, shine! thy might is passed;
        the glory of the Lord hath risen upon thee,
            GOD is thy glory, thy life, thine all."

IV

CREED

AND THE CHRISTIAN YEAR

THY GOD THY GLORY

SHEW me, O GOD most holy,
    according to the measure of our mortal sight,
        THY GLORY.
Disclose the splendours of thy power, thy wisdom, and
        thy love,
    as the new sun breaks upon the night shadows
      and day leaps into joy.

But day is here! thy glory thou hast revealed
    already, wonderfully, if we will but see;
glory, more glorious than might or majesty
    or any magnificence of imagined heaven,
in the face of a little Child, thy Son, my Christ,
    the whole effulgence of thy glory:
    come that men might call thee FATHER
      and be called thy sons:

the glory of One despised and rejected of men,
    dying without the gates,
who has washed us clean from our sins in his own blood
      to make us priests and kings:

the glory of the Living One, Beginning and End of all,
    the image of the invisible GOD,
  shining as the sun shines in strength,
freely imparting to us the Spirit of his glory
    that we may live and not die.

O GOD, most glorious,
    make our life the vision of thee
      to the praise of thy glory;
    that we all as a mirror may reflect it,
    and be transformed into the same image
      from glory to glory,
          world without end.

CREATION

O LORD CREATOR,
    thou that madest all things that were made,
    thou that makest all things new:

enable us thy creatures
    to CREATE according to thy life in us,
             according to thy power in us,
             according to thy love in us:

in thy Name and by thine operation—
    to create good by firm adherence to thy will;
    to build holiness by prayer;
    to uplift justice and integrity in all our dealings;
    to bless men by serving them;
    to heal both by faith and works;
    to fashion beauty of scene and soul;
    to magnify truth by contemplating, interpreting, and
          proclaiming it;
    to beget joy by dwelling in thy Presence;
    to quicken love by thy Holy Spirit;
    to ensue thy peace
          and to publish thy glory—

whose is the Majesty, Dominion, and Power,
    world without end. Amen.

THE CREATOR

GOD MADE goodness, not we:
　　grant us, O Lord, to pursue it.
　God made truth, not we:
　　grant us, Lord, to search it out.
　God made beauty, not we:
　　grant us, Lord, to perceive it.
　God made love, not we:
　　pour, Lord, thy love into our hearts
　　　more and more abundantly.

With all these wonders thou dost dazzle our eyes
　　　and fill our hands.
And each is inexhaustible; and all
　　thou hast manifested before our eyes
　　　in Jesus Christ our Lord;
　　and dost offer to us
　　　by thy Holy Spirit.

Yet more;
　　thou madest life, not we:
　　thou madest us, not we ourselves;
in thee we live and move and have our being,
　　without thee, we are not.

And most;
　　　thou madest us for communion with thee;
what thou hast offered, may we not refuse;
　　what thou hast given, let us not throw away.
Dear Lord, thou givest all;
　　but askest all.

As the young king asked wisdom, so do we ask faith
　　to grow into thy goodness,
　　　into thy truth, thy beauty, thy love
　　　　into THYSELF.

THE DIVINE MAJESTY

I

SHEW me thy majesty, O Lord God
the majesty of thy glory,
but once, but for an instant,
and it suffices.

YET shewn it, thou hast:
    not once, nor twice,
    not for a moment, nor an hour, nor a day,
       but hourly, daily, always;
shewn not one, but many majesties
       unsearchable, inexpressible,
       majesty upon majesty and the fulness of glory,
    IN JESUS CHRIST THY SON OUR LORD.

IN JESUS CHRIST, THY SON, OUR LORD:
    whom having seen, we have seen the Father:
    whom seeing, we see GOD:
    whom we may not only see,
       but know, and accompany, and love:
who chooses and comes to dwell among us,
    to make his abode in us,
       full of grace and truth.

O LORD GOD, Son of the Father, everlasting WORD,
    thou dost reveal the divine MAJESTY
    in whatsoever thou didst speak, do, and suffer,
       the whole and very Majesty of GOD:
the Majesty of humility,
    that laid thee in a manger,
    and let the Cross be laid upon thee,
       meek and lowly of heart;
the Majesty of faith,
    who gavest the Father the whole trust of a human
       heart,
    alike in mighty works and the assumption of
       shame;
Majesty in suffering,
    who when they reviled, smote, scourged,
       didst not murmur, but prayed
    for them that nailed thy hands and feet;
the Majesty of love,
    who, when thou lovest, lovest unto the end,
    when thou forgivest, blottest out the whole,
    when thou givest, givest all,
       givest thyself;
the Majesty of triumph,
    who by death didst destroy death
       and the power of sin;
    and by a perfect life, livest ever,
       King of kings and Lord of lords.

O glorious Lord, who still dost descend to us,
    grant us by communion with thee
       the sight and knowledge of thy Majesty;
       and, by dwelling in thee,
         ascension into it.

FOUNTAIN OF LIFE

O MY GOD, from thee I proceed;
    to thee I belong;
        thee adore.

Thou art the Fountain of my whole being
    Fountain of a thousand springs
        of mercy, pardon, and loving kindness;
    Source of light, Well of grace;
        thee I adore.

Thine is the voice of many waters
        now loud, now low, and lovely always,
    calling me to thy work and mine,
    calling to faith, to hope, to resolve,
    calling to love, the greatest of these;
        thee I adore.

Fountain of joy and melody in the heart,
    Fountain of peace and quietness of soul,
    Fountain of will to do thy will,
        thee I adore.

Spring and Fountain and River and Flood,
    O GOD most holy,
        from thee I proceed,
        to thee I belong,
    my Beginning, my Goal, my All,
        thee I adore.

THE BLESSED VIRGIN

HAIL MARY, full of grace,
thou hast found favour with God.

LET US, with the Great Angel,
    salute in gratitude and joy
        out sister and Mother in Jesus.

Blessed be she among women,
    whose womb bore God's Son.
Blessed by God's grace be we all,
    that He should make His body of hers.

Blessed be she who obeyed:
    I am the bondmaid of the Lord;
    as He has said, so be it.
And blessed all who do His will
    humbly, joyfully, as she.

No sooner had she spoken it,
    than the overshadowing of the Holy Ghost
        formed Christ within.
By thy same Holy Spirit, O God,
    conceive in us thy whole will,
        thine own life.

O Power of the Most High,
    who, for our sake, came upon Mary,
        come upon us!

BE IT UNTO ME
ACCORDING TO THY WORD

FIAT mihi secundum verbum tuum.

LORD, when daily thine angel cometh to me,
 messenger of immortal grace,
 summoner to mortal choice,
let me daily expect thy divine word,
 and learn by thy divine light
  to accept and to perform thy will.
Fiat mihi secundum verbum tuum.

Give me grace
 to abandon myself,
  to obey thee joyfully and promptly,
  to serve thy sure design,
   and to finish my calling,
Even as Mary, maiden and mother,
 accepted all, surrendered all, completed all;
—and unto us a Child was born,
 unto us a Son is given;
 whose Name is called Wonderful,
 Counsellor, the Mighty God, the Prince of Peace,
  henceforth even for ever.

DOMINE Deus,
 fiat mihi secundum verbum tuum.

OBUMBRA ME ALTISSIME

OVERSHADOW me, O Most High, with thy Holy Spirit,
    and, as in Mary, Mother of Jesus, Mother of saints,
        Mother of joy to a lost world,
            grant thy Son may be born in me.

Lord God, above and beneath every cloud
        sweeping over the hour or day,
    make me aware of thy Holy Spirit
        coming with the brightness of heaven,
            to kindle holy life within me;
    transforming the shadows of doubtfulness into a
            radiance,
        the shadows of care and pain into peace,
        the shadows of common concerns
            into the fuel of heavenly love.

O Lord Christ, send me not with the proud empty away;
        be born in me, abide in me:
        be born as a babe, that I may be lowly,
    be born as a master, whom I will obey,
    be born as a saviour, that I may give thanks,
        and grow into thy likeness,
           reflecting thy truth and thy praise
                now and for ever.

CHRISTMAS EVE.

MARY, in the days of her holy expectation,
  magnified the Lord;
 her spirit rejoiced in the child of her womb,
  the Son of God.

For when all things lay in silence,
  and night was in the midst of her course,
there leaped down, O God, from on high,
  from thy royal throne,
   the Word, thy Christ, thyself;
  through woman to be born in human nature,
   born in time, born in us,
   and we in him.

Grant me, O God, thy divinest gift,
  that Emmanuel may be formed and born in me,
  and I may ever rejoice and magnify thee.
Say to my soul, Peace, be still,
   as was that silent night.
And send thy Word, into my soul,
  not for my merit, but by thy miracle;
  by my desire, but of thy sole gift;
  not in part, but in all
   which mortal can receive.

Father, let me be born in thee as thy child:
Christ, be born in me as my Lord:
Holy Spirit, travail and shine within;
  that I may live in thy life
  and love with thy love
   evermore and evermore.

INCARNATION

What is man that thou visitest him,
and the son of man that thou so regardest him?

LORD, let me kneel before thy miracle.
  —an infant in a stable
    on a human mother's breast,
  from all eternity thine only begotten Son,
    thy Word from before beginning,
  God of God, Light of Light, Very God of
                                    Very God,
      of his own choice, of thine own purpose,
        made mortal man.

What is man that thou visitest him,
and the son of man that thou so regardest him?

O CHRIST, let me kneel before the wonder of thy Glory
      thus made manifest to all flesh;
  to be made one with thy lowliness,
        one with thine obedience,
        one with thy majesty of love,
  in a union, that by thy grace
        shall know no divorce
          unto the ages of ages. Amen.

BETHLEHEM

GLORIA IN EXCELSIS DEO

WHAT is this wonder which openeth the heavens
    with hosts and hymns of angels?
Who is this babe, rough-lying in the straw
    beside the cattle?
And who this infant, born of a woman,
    to whom shepherds and kings kneel?

This is a Shepherd, the chief Shepherd, the good Shepherd,
    Shepherd of all mankind,
      who giveth his life for the sheep.
And this a King, the King of kings,
    sovereign of all souls,
      whose kingdom can have no end.
Who in the day of eternity and splendour
    subsisted in the Form of GOD;
yet chose the bitterness of a mortal lot
  for us, for me,
THE LORD GOD ALMIGHTY,
    my Shepherd, my King, my all.

Let us also go unto Bethlehem
    singing the hymn of knowledge
        and of adoration.

GLORIA IN EXCELSIS DEO

JESUS IS COME

JESUS IS COME—
    the Word of GOD hath spoken it:
first to Mary by the tongue of her travail,
to Joseph next in the night-visions,
to poor shepherds by a chorus of angels,
to the wise and wealthy through the shining of a star,
    to the whole world by a Babe.

The Word of GOD hath spoken it,
  JESUS IS COME—
to save the pitiful lost sons of men;
    save, by the glory of a lowly life,
        which all eyes should see;
    save, by the voice of truth,
        which all ears may hear;
    save, by the compassion of a heart,
        which we pierced.

The Word of GOD, HIMSELF, hath spoken it,
  JESUS, SAVIOUR, IS COME
        that we might have life
          more and more abundantly,
  His infinite lowliness hath exalted us,
his infinite love forgiven and renewed,
his infinite majesty summoned us
      to an infinite hope and crown.

JESUS IS COME—
    who is over all, God, blessed for ever.

THE DIVINE SURPRISES

BLESSED be thou, O Lord God,
            for the Surprises of Truth.
Blessed thou who now as of old
            dost come suddenly into thy temple,
        to make thine abode with us,
           and all things new.

New every day is the Surprise
        that thou, God of all that is,
            shouldest call me son,
           and thyself my Father.
Surprise, to mark thy hand at my helm always.
           down the sea of years.

Surprise, beyond conceiving,
        thy grace to one and all
            once shewn, perpetually given:
the advent of a human Babe;
        the spending once, the dispensing ever,
           of his Body and Blood;
his lifting up to die,
        to draw all men to himself,
            yet never to depart from them;
the Son, whom having seen we have seen thee,
           O Father.

Every day thou dost come into thy temple
           suddenly, silently,
bringing thy truth, thy joy, thy might,
           thy Spirit, thy self;
deigning to love us within us,
        so that by thee we may worship thee
           in spirit and in truth.

ΣHMEION—SIGNIFICATIO

O LORD JESUS CHRIST, we bless, we adore thee
    for all thou wert, and didst enact, on earth, in time.
Never man spake as thou didst speak:
    thou wentest about doing only good.
All that thou didst say, and work, and suffer,
    is both fact that was and truth that is,
        truth to all ages, truth for all souls,
            the sign once, the signification perpetual:
    all, all, is timeless.

That was the true Light coming into the world,
    opening, for ever, the eyes of the blind.
The heart of the Eternal beat in a human heart;
    a human beats in heaven.
When thou feddest the multitude,
    thou feddest mankind;
thine own prayer pleads on innumerable lips;
thine own wounds forgive, heal, comfort, day and night;
the life thou tookest back to thyself
    imparts our immortality.

Lord, in that life lived on our earth,
    full human, all divine,
    thou wert one with the Father;
one light, one fire, one love, one breath,
one glory, visible yet surpassing sight,
    GOD, and the voice of God to man,
        for evermore.

So, Lord, we adore, we bless thee
    in the mystery of thy holy Incarnation,
    in thy Word of power and healing,
    in thy most holy Cross,
    in thy glorious Resurrection,
    in thy Reign of Grace,
        world without end. Amen.

GETHSEMANE

WHILE THY best friends slept
    thou didst work their salvation.
Day in, day out, O Lord Christ
    thou dost work ours,
        while we too sleep.

Thou, O Son of man, Son of God,
    in the Garden, at the Pillar, on the Cross
didst take away the sin of the world,
    and its darkness, and its death;
thyself bearing the cost
    in thine own body and mind and soul,
        all human, all divine.

Yet we sleep. Come, Lord, and wake us
    from the absorptions and the stupor of self-will.
Grant us to heed the tender warning,
    Why sleep ye? Rise and pray,
        lest ye enter into temptation.
And still thou speakest to each,
    From all eternity I have loved thee;
    thee to all eternity will I love;
        canst thou not spare me one hour?

Lead us forward to watch and pray with thee
    to do the will of the Father,
    to shew the courage of a son of God,
    to share by thy great grace, O Lord,
that work of thine, that love, that suffering,
    that holy Spirit
        which redeems.

THE KING

BEHOLD YOUR KING!
He comes, long hope of the prophets,
    Desire of all nations,
    Lord of the world, of all worlds—
        comes to his own.

Behold your King—he is here!
The Church, the High Priest, asks him,
    Art thou the Christ?
        And he said, I AM.
The State, the Governor, the Judge asks him
    Art thou a King then?
        I AM.
The people of God acclaim him,
His blood be upon us and on our children:
    we have no king but Caesar:
        crucify him.

King will he call himself?
    Give him a stalk for sceptre,
    Cover his gashes with a regal robe,
        crown him with thorns!
    Set him on high to reign,
    Fasten him there with nails,
        watch him die!

This is the Bible King:
    this the mystery of Truth:
this the immeasurable measure of Love:
    the eternal Glory:
        GOD.

INVENTION OF THE HOLY CROSS

O SAVIOUR LORD, crucified for me,
    crucified by me,
attach me to the long line of pilgrims
    who have sought and discovered the True Cross:
—not the old worn wood, but its living grace;
—not the cruel relic of a bygone woe,
    but the wisdom of God for the mind,
    the power of God for the will,
    the patience of God towards our angers and ignorances,
        thy generosity unto death.

By the very depth, dear Lord, of their abasement
    thy pains for us were divine;
        humbly we thank thee.
The very height, dear Lord, of human exaltation
    man has found in suffering for thy Name;
        humbly we thank thee.

The True Cross is found
    when we resist, striving against sin,
        even unto blood.
The True Cross is lifted up
    in our obedience as sons,
    in our fellowship with thy sufferings,
        in faithfulness to the end.
The True Cross is adored
    if the world be crucified to me,
        and I to the world;
    if I may bear in my body
        the marks of the Lord Jesus.

Grant, Lord, that as the True Cross
    was, is, and ever shall be thy Glory,
        so it may be mine.

AVE CRUX

THOU ART welcome, Holy Cross of our GOD!
    Thou bringest light:
    thou shewest the wisdom of GOD and the power
        of GOD.

Thou bringest love;
    for so GOD loved the world
    that he gave his only-begotten Son
    to bear thee and to be borne by thee.

Thou bringest life,
    on whom the Saviour is lifted up to die
      and to draw all men unto him.

Thou bringest freedom and forgiveness,
    through the nails which held thy Lord to thee,
    through the precious Blood
      which angels gathered and men drink.

Thou hast set a throne on the soil of our earth
    whereon men can see the heart of GOD,
      and bow and adore.

LORD JESUS, let me not fear nor hesitate to take from thy
        hands
    the disciple's cross;
and carry it, whatsoever its weight or pain,
    with all the sons of faith.
Let me follow the Master's way and the Master's will,
    to thy goal, thy glory.

PRAYER BENEATH THE CROSS

MY GOD, MY FATHER, help me to pray
WITH JESUS ON THE CROSS.

By praying for any enemies
who wish me hurt;
and more, for thine,
who do injustice and cruelty on the earth.
Father, forgive them, for they know not what they do.

By praying for the guilty and condemned,
WITH JESUS ON THE CROSS:
for all facing trial or in prison,
and all captives of sin:
bring them to look up to his holy Cross:
and, hand in hand with him, go free.

By praying for the grace of love in human homes:
for heavenly concord in thy household, the Church,
born of Christ's blood:
praying with Jesus, with his Mother, with St John,
for love, for holier love, on earth.

By holding fast to thee, my God, my God,
who holdest fast to us,
in the black and desperate day
and in the hour of death.

By praying, O Eternal Compassion,
　　for all in pain of body or mind:
　　for souls that thirst for thee:
　　and souls that wander in dry places,
　　　　seeking rest, but not seeking thee.

By praying for the present help of thine own Spirit,
　　that all thou givest me to do
　　　　may be fearlessly begun,
　　　　and faithfully finished.

So help me God to pray WITH JESUS ON THE CROSS
　　and to commend my body, mind, and spirit,
　　O Father, into thy hands
　　　　for life, for death, for time without end.

ELOI ELOI

THERE, where was the frame of an infant,
  the limbs of a lad,
    the mature mind of a man,
There, from cradle to tomb, dwelt GOD.

There, on human lips, from a human heart,
    spoke the WORD OF GOD.
There, beyond the compass of a created soul,
      moved the uncreate SPIRIT OF GOD.

And there he hung, scorned and dying,
    on the abominable cross
      where we set him.
Yet there, and thence for ever, he proclaims
    the irrefutable, irresistible GOSPEL OF GOD,
      calling mankind, calling me:
— summoning us to undying victory
    along roads where no trumpets sound,
      nor temporal profits count,
      but FAITH only, and faithfulness unto death;
        ELOI, ELOI.

O my Lord, lead me safe through all the tests,
    the darknesses, the pains.
Help me hold fast the beginning of my confidence
    firm unto the end.
ELOI, ELOI, stretch forth thy wounded hands
    to succour mine.
Never wilt thou forsake me,
    never let me forsake thee,
      my living, only GOD.

EASTER

THOU ART RISEN, O LORD!
  Let the gospel trumpets speak,
  and the news as of holy fire,
      burning and flaming and inextinguishable,
        run to the ends of the earth.

THOU ART RISEN, O LORD!
  Let all creation greet the good tidings
        with jubilant shout;
      for its redemption has come,
      the long night is past, the Saviour lives!
      and rides and reigns in triumph
        now and unto the age of ages.

THOU ART RISEN, O LORD!
  Let the quiet Altar dazzle with light;
      let us haste to thy Presence
      wondering, incredulous for joy;
        and partake of thy Risen Life.

THOU ART RISEN, MY LORD AND MY GOD!
  Rise up, my heart, give thanks, rejoice!
  And do thou, O Lord, deign to enter it
        despite the shut doors.
  Shew me thy hands and thy side,
        that it is thou thyself.
  Send me about thy business,
      servant of the living King, the King of kings;
      and hide my life in thine
        for ever and ever.

ASCENSION

O RISEN SAVIOUR, bid me rise with thee
  and seek those things which are above;
  not only seek, but set my whole heart upon them.

Thou art in heaven, ever raising lives to thyself;
  O, by thy grace, may mine be making that ascent
      not in dream, but in truth,
      now, to-morrow, always.

Daily in spirit, in thy Holy Spirit,
  let me behold thee on the throne of GOD,
      thou King reigning in holiness,
      thou Conqueror of all evil,
      thou Majesty of love,
      very GOD and very Man,
  of glory unimaginable and eternal,
      in whom all hope is sure.

So, longing for thy courts,
      let me rise, ascend, seek;
  finding in the nearer light of thy countenance
      higher and yet higher things
      to love, to do, and to attain.

Until, through the open door of heaven,
  that most blessed voice shall speak;
  "Enter thou into thy Lord's joy",
      and thy servant comes—
  to sing of thy glory and honour all the day long
  and tell of all thy wondrous works;
      knowing no end thereof,
      for there is no end thereof.

THE LAST ACCOUNT

O LORD GOD, the Ancient of Days,
    for the mortal term which thy bounty giveth
        thou bringest every son into account.
To each thou dost entrust the talents and pounds
    to employ unto the reckoning.

O most merciful, most just,
    grant us while it is called to-day,
        the day's grace for the day's work.
For now is the time to win our acceptance,
    now is the day of salvation.

Grant that we stand not idle as the hours pass:
    set us to labour in thy vineyard,
        until the night come when no man can work.

New every morning are thy mercies,
    new and sure and full.
Withhold not from me, O my God, the best,
    the Spirit of thy dear Son;
that in that Day when the judgment is set
    I may be presented unto thee
        not blameless, but forgiven,
        not effectual but faithful,
        not holy but persevering,
        without desert but accepted,
because he hath pleaded the causes of my soul,
    and redeemed my life.

DOOMSDAY

LORD GOD, at that great and last assize,
    thou wilt search out with light and fire
        them that have loved Jesus
           and with him obeyed thy will.

Many mistakes will they have made
           and have fallen often,
will have seen but dimly, misunderstood,
           denied, betrayed—
but they have believed and sought and loved thy Son,
           have knelt by his Cross,
    and after disobedience, mourned and turned again.

The Spirit of thy love, sharp as a sword,
    will pierce to the dividing asunder of true and false;
and disentangle the honest heavenly desire in us
    from the toys and covetings of common day
        and from the swellings of self.

O grant me thine absolution, O Lord, now, to-day,
    let thy fire consume the dross, the mortal, the vain;
        thy light kindle my love,
           infant but immortal.

O feed my heart's longing!
    strengthen and confirm my love;
that the eternal may swallow up the temporal, even now;
    and in that last hour I may stand before thee
        sorry, ashamed, trembling,
           but in hope.

GOD THE HOLY GHOST

O MOST HOLY SPIRIT, thou comest,
     as once came Christ to Bethlehem,
        to a most mean dwelling, even to me.
But thou canst cleanse and make it a temple,
     THY temple, full with holiness, love, and joy.

So come, O Spirit of GOD,
        with GOD the Father's love;
        by Christ's Body and Blood;
        in the new birth of thine own breath.
Come to cover my littlenesses and consume my sins,
        to direct all my desires and doings;
come with counsel on my perplexities,
        with light from thine everlasting scriptures;
come to reveal the deep things of GOD,
        and what he prepareth for them that love him;
come with thy prayer into mine.

O most Holy Spirit,
     possess me by thy peace,
     illuminate me by the truth,
     fire me by thy flame,
     enable me by thy power,
     be made visible in me by thy fruits,
     lift me by grace upon grace
        from glory to glory,
     O Spirit of the Lord;
who art with the Father and the Son one GOD,
        world without end.

THE SPIRIT OF LIFE

I

BLESSED Spirit of God,
    pour upon us such gifts of faith, purity, and love,
    that we may have thy temple within us,
        and thee in that temple
        and life everlasting in thee;
    through Jesus Christ our Lord.

II

O HOLY GHOST,
        giver of light and life;
Impart to us thoughts higher than our own thoughts,
    and prayers better than our own prayers,
    and powers beyond our own powers;
that we may spend and be spent
        in the ways of love and goodness,
    after the perfect image
        of our Lord and Saviour Jesus Christ.

III

SPIRIT calls to spirit—
        Know me as I know thee;
        Seek me as I seek thee;
        Claim me as I claim thee;
Learn my love that thou mayest love;
Choose my will that thou mayest live,
        And take my life to do it.

And spirit answers Spirit—
O Lord I am a child that has no knowledge,
So teach me:
And blind and see not the way,
So lead me:
And weak, most weak, to choose aright,
So supply thy power:
And love myself too well,
So shew me, give me, love,
true love, THYSELF.

HOLY CHURCH

LORD GOD, thou hast built in heaven and earth
a single Church
of Truth and Love and holy Spirit;
one family and communion, whose temple is the Lamb,
one body indivisible, here and beyond,
the Body of thy dear Son.

Thou art its foundation and corner-stone, thou its head
and life,
O JESUS EMMANUEL;
thou, whom we have seen and touched and know,
eternal Truth, eternal Love, holy and eternal Spirit.

Who is like GOD? Does GOD build upon the sand?
Against God's mind, against God's Church,
what can prevail?
Who can contract its bounds? who divide the Divine?
Not mortal men on its temporal fringes,
not we who crucify Christ.

The unity of holy Church, its might, its gospel,
proceeding each from GOD's unalterable will,
is Truth and Love and holy Spirit.
Its ministries, O GOD, stream from thy heart,
Truth, Love, and holy Spirit, one and all.
There is no other Truth than thine, nor can be such a Love,
and all made ours within one family, one Father's House,
one Vine, one Bread and Cup, one Body.

Father, all souls are thine: gather them into one;
bring us into the one Truth;
bind us by the one Love;
perfect us with the one Spirit;
pity our senile schisms, heal the long hates of death;
within thy single Church built of thy grace,
grant us thy peace.

THE COMMUNION OF SAINTS

THOU ART to be praised in all thy saints;
    honoured and blessed and magnified in each.
THOU didst foreknow them before the beginning of time;
    even then were they thy beloved.
THOU didst choose them out of the world;
    and call them by grace
    and draw them with the cords of love.
THOU didst bring them safe through divers temptations,
    through fire and water and the provings of sorrow.
THOU didst supply them with glorious consolations,
    lead them out into a wealthy place,
    and crown their patience.
THOU didst raise their will and their life unto thee,
    by the breath and flame of thy Holy Spirit.
THOU dost unite them in one,
    and clothe them with light and joy as with a garment.

Now they follow the Lamb whithersoever he goeth,
    and fall before thy throne,
        who livest for ever and ever.

O Lord, into this happy, blessèd, glorious society,
        inseparable from thee,
grant admission even now to us
    who have been grafted into the Church of thy dear Son;
    and at the last number us with them
        in glory everlasting.

ALL SAINTS

O LORD GOD, though I be yet upon this earth,
    let me live in the company of thy crownéd saints;
making melody in my heart with them,
singing from my soul their jubilant song,
        Alleluia, Alleluia.

They, O Christ, have beauty
        which this world never could create;
they have accomplished what is above human strength;
they shine with light unchanging, timeless, wonderful.
For they gave themselves unto thee
        and received from thee;
    and shine with thy loveliness
    and are thine for ever,
        Alleluia, Alleluia.

Do you, great friends, great fellowship of God,
        praise God on my behalf,
    so low, so little is my own power of praise.
You who were penitent and watched in prayer,
        laboured, held fast, and overcame,
        lend to my would-be praises the voice of yours!
You, whose days were humbly hid in Jesus,
        who kept his words and works unto the end,
            you who were faithful unto death;
You, clothed now in white raiment
        and crowned with life;
You, going forth conquering and to conquer
        after the King of kings—
cry out for all the heavens, for all Holy Church,
        and for me, a sinner,
        Alleluia, Alleluia.

ST PETER

PRAISED be St Peter, the glorified of God,
      chief, O Christ, of thine apostles,
fisherman of souls, martyr of the Faith,
      brother of ours:
whom out of weakness, thou madest a ROCK
      and on it built thy Church.

If ever I would deny thee, Lord,
      grant me his prayers.
When I have denied thee, O Lord,
      grant me his tears.

Grant me, with him, to know that I love thee.
Grant me his call, to feed thy sheep.
Grant me his courage, even to rejoice
      in suffering shame or pain
         for thy sake.
Grant me in the end his glory,
      thy crowning.

St Peter, Christ's Rock, pray for me,
      in the days of my discipleship,
      in the house of my faith,
         in the hour of my death.

ST PAUL

BLESSED BE GOD for St Paul,
    the converted, the called, the chosen of Christ:

  Converted, wonderfully, from blindness and error,
    from bigotry and hate,
        to the illuminations of faith,
        to the slavery of love.

  Called, wonderfully, to the preaching of God's Gospel,
    ambassador to the nations
        through labours and watchings,
        in strifes and imprisonments,
    by perils in city and wilderness and sea,
        for the Name of the Lord Jesus.

  Chosen, wonderfully, to learn and impart
    the wisdom of the Cross
        and the power of the Resurrection,
    the forgiveness of sin and our new creation,
        the gifts and indwelling of the Holy Ghost;
    and to bear in body and in soul
        the marks of the Lord Jesus.

Blessed be God for St Paul!
For the good fight he fought,
    and the truth that he taught
        blessed be God!

Apostle, ambassador, martyr, and saint,
        plead for us, plead with us,
    that Christ may dwell in our hearts by faith;
    that we also may press towards the goal
        of the high calling of God in Christ Jesus:
and be made conformable
    to his death, to his life,
        to his glory.

ST JAMES THE GREAT

PRAISED be St James, the glorified of God!

LORD, grant me the prayers of St James,
   disciple and friend whom thou didst choose,
   son of thunder, fisher of men,
   eyewitness of thy majesty,
     first martyr apostle.

Grant me his prayer,
   that my faith may become as complete,
     aflame, and fearless as his
   who was baptized with thine own baptism,
     and drank of thy cup.

O Lord, for the love of St James,
     purge my ambitions;
   that I see at no time first place
     nor any good thing for myself,
   except to be servant of all
     by serving thee.

Grant me to drink of whatever cup
     thou wilt appoint.
Bring me by grace to thy kingdom
     thy way, not mine.

St James, great martyr of Christ,
     pray for me
   in the days of my discipleship,
   in the house of my faith,
     in the hour of my death.

ST JOHN'S SERMON

ST JOHN in his old age, day after day,
                again and again,
        preached one sermon, in one sentence,
Little children, love one another.

For, *love is of God,* and *God is love,*
and the Master's own commandment final,
        Love one another
                        as I have loved you.

Every day, every hour, Lord Jesus,
        keep us in this one obedience,
to learn love, create love, dispense love,
        live love behind both act and impulse
                and in all our intercourse;
a reverent love, thoughtful and wide and happy,
        unsparing of self and labour;
imitators of thee, disciples of love,
                Christlike.

But that we may love others, O Lord Christ,
        lead us first, lead us always, to love GOD.
Fill our minds with thy mind, and majesty, of love;
hold thine incarnate life of love
                before our eyes;
hide the wounds of thy love
                within our heart;
that, loving thee with all our strength,
        our love may flow as a mighty stream
                through thyself
        to all whom thou lovest.

ST JOHN

PRAISED be St John, the glorified of God!

LORD, grant me the prayers of St John,
    disciple and friend whom thou lovest,
    apostle of love, thy love, for ever,
        eternal evangelist:

that my faith may become as complete,
    as flaming and tranquil, as his,
    and pierce as deep,
    and speak as simply
        in the Spirit.
that I may apprehend thee as Light
    lighting every man,
        every creature and every thing,
        every moment.
that I may know thee as Truth,
    hearing thy voice;
that I may serve thee as Love,
    loving the brethren;
    asking for no reward, no place,
    but one only and for one instant—
        to lean on thy bosom.

St John, on Christ's bosom,
        pray for me
    in the days of my discipleship,
    in the house of my faith,
    in the hour of my death.

THE FAITHFUL DEPARTED

ARE we to mourn our dead, our beloved,
  as men that have no hope?

THOU, O GOD, art not GOD of the dead,
    but of the living.
In thy resurrection, O Christ, we celebrate ours.
The gift of thy life, O Holy Spirit, is not for a season,
    but for ever.

As long as thou art with thy servants, thy children,
    they are with thee; they lose nothing by dying.
They depart out of the world, but not out of thy family.
They vanish from our sight, but not from thy care.
One sun hath set upon them, but a greater is risen.
They are not dead; nay, it is death that hath died in them;
    their death that is buried in their grave.
They leave behind the mortal, to put on immortality;
    theirs is entrance into healing, into rest, into glory.

LORD, thou hast made, endowed, redeemed, employed
                thy children,
    thou canst not desert nor annihilate them,
    canst not but be gracious eternally.
Thou forgettest not the dead whom we forget;
    thou rewardest the benefactors we never knew.
Thou who holdest worlds in life
    holdest them.

O FATHER, O Saviour, O Giver of Life,
    by thy mercy, thine unalterable love,
gather thy sons and daughters together unto thyself,
    those who have taken thee for their strength,
    those who have served thee with sacrifice,
    those who have offered thee thanks and praise.
May they rejoice in the Jerusalem of grace and peace,
    and praise thee among the choirs of the blessèd,
                in joy without end.

THE LIFE

THOU art the Life, O Christ.
    It was the Prince of Life that we slew,
        the King that liveth for ever,
        the First and the Last and the Living One;
    who wouldest be the Life of all,
        the death of none.

Grant us, O Lord, to lay hold on life
        by faith in thee,
        by good works wrought through thee;
    who camest that we might have life
        ever more and more abundantly.

This is the day which the Lord hath made,
        the day of Life;
    let me rejoice and be glad in it.
Let me be better to-day than yesterday,
        and better to-morrow than to-day.
For thou hast set before us life and good,
        and death and evil—
let me choose good, let me choose THEE,
        that I may live.

THE HEAVENLY CITY

O MY GOD,
    bring me, even now, to the mansions
    which thy Son prepareth for them that love thee.
Every day make me to dwell in the eternal,
    and live unto thee.

Let me walk in that heavenly city
    of which the Lamb is the light:
let me serve as in the courts
    where the Lamb reigneth:
let me follow the Lamb
    whithersoever he goeth:
and fear not, cease not, to battle for right
    after the King of kings and Lord of lords.

Let my conversation be in heaven
    with thy blesséd and beloved,
        the whole company of the redeemed;
    and with hierarchies of angels
praising, worshipping, and adoring him
    that sitteth upon the throne
        for ever and ever.

V

EUCHARISTIC DEVOTIONS

THE MEETING PLACE

WHEN I pray in my chamber,
    I build a sanctuary there.
When I cast out a prayer upon the street,
    a spire rises suddenly to the skies.
When, without voice, my soul prays in any place,
    my whole being becomes a church.
When my faith kindles and flames into praise
      the whole created world becomes a Minster.

Yet none of these were temples
          except GOD come to it;
     and come he will, if I so build.
But how much more shall he not come
        to the Altar himself has built?
      whither he has invited, nay bidden us
        to meet him?
     where he has set out the feast
     and provided his Life for food,
       his Passion for drink?

Here is the temple of temples
        the holy of holies,
     himself the light, himself the altar,
     himself the host, himself the feast.
Here let devotions rise up like incense,
      here union and communion be made with God,
     be his abiding here with us
       and ours in HIM.

Blessed is he that cometh in the Name of the Lord;
   Hosanna in the highest.

APPROACH

LORD, I am come into thy House:
    to seek thy love as Father
        and my heavenly clothing as son:
    to seek thy bidding as my GOD
        and thy power to do it;
    to seek the glory of thy Presence
        and the breath of thy Holy Spirit:
    to seek the likeness of thy Christ
        and his very Life.

I will come in upon thy great goodness,
    and set my heart upon thy light and truth,
        and wait upon thy pleasure;
yea, Lord I will seek thee and thy strength
    and thy face evermore.

Lord, be merciful to me, a sinner:
    cast me not away from thy Presence.
Make me a clean heart, O GOD,
    and renew a right spirit within me.
So will I go to the mercy-seat of thy holy temple;
    where all who seek, find,
    and all who find, abide,
        in peace, in thee.

THE GIVER

O LORD, my Father and GOD,
    thou art the Giver of all good gifts.
In all that thou givest—and always thou givest—
    thou givest only the good.
Though it come through adversity, vexation, sorrow,
      make me to apprehend that good,
          the wisdom of thy law,
             the height and depth of thy love;
     apprehend, accept, give thanks.

Nay, in all that thou givest,
      thou givest, not the good, but the best;
         nothing less wouldest thou give,
         nothing else canst thou give;
    and that best is THYSELF,
        nothing less, nothing else:

THYSELF given once and wholly in thy Son,
THYSELF given always and without measure in thy Spirit,
THYSELF given visibly in thy Sacrament,
        invisibly everywhere,
     unfailingly, illimitably, unalterably,
       world without end.

PRAEPARATIO

GRANT us, O Lord GOD,
      to approach thine altar;
and with the whole fellowship of thy redeemed
      to offer and to partake.

Grant us to do thee honour and worship
      with exceeding humility,
      with suppliant reverence,
      with holy intention,
      with faith full and aflame:

Grant us to seek part and abode in Christ,
      in his Truth,
      in his Love,
      in his Life;
which all are eternal, and all Himself;
      who liveth and reigneth with thee and the Holy
        Ghost,
          one GOD, world without end.

WASH ME THROUGHLY

AT THE BIDDING of thy mercy
   O Saviour, O Lord,
  I come to make holy Offering unto the Father
    and to receive thy Body and thy Blood.
But wash me, Saviour; cleanse me, Lord,
  that I may come
    whiter than snow.

Once, before their first Communion,
   thou didst gird thyself with a towel
    and wash thy disciples' feet.
the sinless Lord of all stooped as a slave
    to cleanse their whole being.

Singly, one by one,
   thou didst make them white and pure,
    and give them part with thyself.

As the holy, venerable hands of the High Priest
   made ready to offer to the Father
   the full, the perfect, the eternal Sacrifice,
    HIMSELF—THYSELF, O Christ—
thou didst purify thy friends,
   that they might share in that Offering
    and build with thee thy Church.

Forgive this would-be disciple also, O Lord,
   that I too may be clean;
    and live for thy truth, thy work:
myself have part in thy building on earth,
   part in thine Offering to heaven;
    part with thee.

A PRIEST'S PRAYERS

1. *BEFORE CELEBRATING*

O LORD JESU CHRIST,
By thy most mighty and tender power,
 Impart to me thy lowliness;
 Impart to me thy purity;
 Impart to me thy strength of prayer;
 Impart to me thy love of the Father;
 Impart to me thy perfect priesthood,
  and thy love of souls,
   O my Lord and GOD.

2. *AFTER CELEBRATING*

O LORD JESU CHRIST,
By thy most mighty and most tender gift,
 Awake in me grace upon grace,
 Awake in me joy upon joy,
 Awake in me thanks upon thanks,
  and praise beyond utterance,
 And make all these to abide and abound in me,
   O my Lord and GOD.

EUCHARIST

THOU who didst appoint an Eucharist,
          a sacrifice of thanksgiving
      to be a perpetual memorial of thy Son's Passion
            and Resurrection,
        and a perpetual gift to us;

Help me to have full share in it
        by my thankfulness,
        mine own thankfulness,
        mine own great thankfulness—
      to GOD the Father, who giveth me his Son,
      to GOD the Son, who giveth me his Spirit,
      to GOD the Spirit who giveth me his Presence
        and Eternity.

Praise the Lord, O my soul;
      and all that is within me
        praise his holy Name.

THE LORD'S SUPPER

LORD, this is thy feast,
        prepared by thy longing,
        spread at thy command,
        attended at thine invitation,
        blessed by thine own Word,
        distributed by thine own hand,
        the undying memorial of thy sacrifice
                upon the Cross,
        the full gift of thine everlasting love,
        and its perpetuation till time shall end.

LORD, this is Bread of heaven,
                Bread of life,
        that, whoso eateth, never shall hunger more.
        And this the Cup of pardon, healing, gladness,
                strength,
        that, whoso drinketh, thirsteth not again.

So may we come, O Lord, to thy Table;
        Lord Jesus, come to us.

THE ETERNAL FEAST

STILL, O LORD, thou dost gather round thyself
      the company of thy friends,
  desiring with eternal desire to sup with them—
         now, when thou reignest,
         as then, before thou didst suffer.

Let me be, O Lord, among their number,
    in the lowest room;
          nay, waiting upon them;
            yet with them, and with thee.

Make me to hunger after the heavenly Food,
        which is THYSELF,
           denied to none that comes.
That life, given for the life of the world,
         mingle now with mine;
        not according to my feeble desire
        but according to thy love.

So shall I live, so shall I love,
        in the company and church of them
     who are for ever gathered round thy table,
       in the eternal mansions,
         in the room of thy heart.

THE CUP OF SACRIFICE

O MY GOD,
      to whom all ages have made sacrifice
      by fruits of the earth, by the blood of beasts, by fire;
help me to know the true and only offering of human kind
      which thou dost desire and wilt accept,
      my faith, my obedience, my love, my life,
         the whole oblation of myself.

O Lord Christ, thou offerest us the Cup,
      which thou thyself didst drink,
         of thine own oblation,
      'the one true pure immortal sacrifice';
      and dost ask of each,
         Art thou able to drink it?

Only, O Lord, if thou wilt cleanse my soul, and clear
         mine eye;
      only if thou wilt draw my heart
         and fill it with thine own Spirit;
      only if thou wilt put with thine own hand
         the cup to my lips,
      and make thine own strength mine.
Then, if I drink, the Passion of my Lord
         shall become mine own oblation;
      his chalice, both my receiving and my gift—
      and that a perfect gift,
         the offering of HIM
            and of myself IN HIM.

PUT ON CHRIST

HELP US, O GOD,
> in the faith of thy holy Apostle, Paul,
> to put on Christ, our Master, thine only-begotten Son:

To put on the robe of his Generosity,
> who for us and for our salvation came down from
> heaven;

the robe of his Purity,
> who was tempted as are we, yet without sin;

the robe of his Obedience,
> whose meat was to do thy will;

the robe of his Humility,
> who was among us as one that serveth;

the robe of his Faith and Courage,
> who, while we were yet in our sins, died for us;

the robe of his Priesthood,
> who bare the sins of many,
> and loveth his own even unto the end:

To put on, O GOD, the mantle of his Wisdom and Power
> by taking up his Cross;

that in the end we may receive the Crown of his award,
> who hath called us to be kings and priests
> unto thee, our GOD and Father;
> to whom be glory and dominion
> for ever and ever.

THE CONSECRATION

THIS IS MY LORD,
     beside and about me,
          coming and entering and abiding within.
This is my Lord, to whom I belong:
This, my Lord, calling me nearer and nearer.

This is my Lord, who died for me:
This, my Lord, who taketh away my sin:
This, my Lord, clothing me in his righteousness:
This, my Lord, giving strength for to-day and to-morrow:
This, my Lord, with his own hands feeding me
          with his own life,
          with his Body and his Blood,
          with his heart and his soul.

As he would dwell in me,
     may I dwell in him
          for ever and ever.

THE CONSECRATION

LORD, THOU ART PRESENT,
    Thou in thy lowliness,
    Thou in thy glory:
Thou that dwellest among us;
Thou whom we refused, wounded, and slew;
Thou, immortal victor, everlasting King:

    Thou our sins' victim;
    Thou my judge;
    Thou mine Advocate
        and voice of my pardon:

    Thou in thy strength;
    Thou in thy tender love;
        Thou with thy heavenly gifts;
        Thou with thy daily calls:

    Thou with thy yielded life,
    Thou with thy living Spirit,
    Thou in thy perfect manhood,
    Thou in thy GODHEAD—
    LORD, thou art here,
        My Food and my Drink
        My Lord and my GOD.

BEHOLD the Body and Blood of my Saviour and Lord!
    Behold whence Love comes forth,
        whence cleansing,
        whence lowliness of heart,
        whence desire and power of oblation,
        whence light, whence wisdom,
        whence joy,
        whence glory and life everlasting—
  from HIM who never ceases to give
        all that he has and is;
  yet reigns with the Father and the Holy Spirit,
        GOD for ever and ever.

GLORIÆ SALVATORIS

A HYMN OF ADORATION

1. LORD that descendedst, Holy Child,
   Dwelling amongst us, Word of God,
      Thee we adore.

2. Jesus our Gospel, Way, and Truth,
   Master and Lover, Light and Life,
      Thee we adore.

3. Saviour uplifted, Man for men,
   Shamed and slaughter'd, Lamb of God,
      Thee we adore.

4. Christ the immortal Risen Lord,
   Christ that ascended, King of kings—
      Thee we adore.

5. Throned in the highest, Very Man,
   Alpha, Omega, God of God,
      Thee we adore.

6. Lord ever-blessed, God most high,
   Lord ever-blessed, God with us,
      Thee we adore.

GRANT me, O Lord Christ,
  growing part with thee, in thee;
    that shall not be taken away.
Part in thy purity,
  in thy courage,
    in thy peace.
Part by forgiving,
  and being forgiven.
Part in thine obedience to the Father's will,
  in thy spirit of love,
  in thy ministries of healing,
  in thy perpetual prayer.
Part in self-offering.
Part in thy sufferings,
    when it be thy call.
Part in thy victory and thy glory,
  who art GOD
      the First and the Last,
        for ever and ever.

AT COMMUNION

Through this blessed Partaking, O Lord,
    restore lost virtues,
            bestow new graces
                by the gift of Thyself.

Blot out past disfigurings,
        fashion new beauty
                by the gift of Thyself.

Disclothe me alike of sloth and busyness,
strip me of pride and love of applause,
clothe me with humility, generosity, and peace
                by the gift of Thyself.

Arm me with thy strength,
        conjoin me to thy victory
                by the gift of Thyself.

Dethrone my self in me;
                O Christ, enthrone Thyself.

LORD, thou hast put gladness in my heart
    satisfying my hunger with good things,
    feeding me with the corn of wheat and very bread
        of heaven,
                even thy Body:

    giving me to drink the wine, which maketh most
        glad the heart of man,
                even thy precious Blood:

    clothing me with the garments of felicity,
                even thy salvation and thy Presence.

    anointing my head with the oil of gladness,
                even the graces of thine all-holy Spirit:

    crowning it with a beautiful crown,
                even the hope of glory,
        that in the dispensation of thy love.
             I shall awake up after thy likeness,
        and be satisfied with it,
             world without end.

AFTER COMMUNION

I GRANT me, O my Father,
    by this grace of thy dear Son
        to live in thy Presence,
            live for thy work,
            live to love;
        now and always.

II O LORD JESUS CHRIST
    wonderful art thou in thy holy places,
    wonderful in thy divine gifts,
    wonderful, most wonderful in the Holy
            Mysteries of thy love—
        commemorating thy death,
        communicating thy life,
    and all thy grace and truth,
        in all ways and for all times.

Thou givest all,
    thou givest Thyself:
    what can I withhold from thee,
        my Lord and my GOD?

AFTER COMMUNION

FATHER,
> who in this Blessed Sacrament
>> hast given us thy Son;
Grant that our persons may be knit to his Person,
> our bodies nourished by his Body,
> our souls washed white by his Blood.

Grant that our whole being may be healed by his wounds,
> hallowed by his touch,
> renewed with holy vows,
>> revivified with his Spirit.

Grant that his Presence may remain
> with its glory and its love
>> and all the blessings of Himself,
> speaking in us and through us;
> fashioning heaven here,
>> and bringing us there hereafter.

VI
ON THE GLORY
AND GOODNESS
OF GOD

GOD

GOD is what thought cannot better;
GOD is whom thought cannot reach;
GOD no thinking can even conceive.
Without God, men can have no being,
    no reason, no knowledge, no good desire, naught.
Thou, O GOD, ART WHAT THOU ART,
    transcending all.

Lord, let us first adore thy transcendent sovereignty,
    else we may never know thy meekness.

Thou art Father, Saviour, Life of life:
thou art majesty most highest:
    thou, in the midst of us;
    thou, he that serveth;
thou our peace, our power, our holiness, our hope;
    leave us not, O Lord our GOD.

Yea, Lord, though our minds must wrestle to the end,
    thinking of thee is more than thought, is peace;
    finding thee more than understanding, is love.
For we have seen thy glory
    and heard the Eternal Word
    and handled the Author of life:
by thy mercy, by thy gift, by thy Son,
    we comprehend thy grace, and receive it,
        grace upon grace.

Blessed be thou, O Lord GOD,
    in the thousand mysteries of thy Word and will,
    in the thousand, thousand wonders of thy love.
Let all mortal flesh keep silence
    and lift itself above all earthly thought,
        kneel and adore.

THY PRESENCE, O God makes Heaven
    and all Heaven's glory is thine own:
thine own joy, thine own honour, thine own blessedness
        create, and are, Heaven.
Before the glory of thy Presence kneel the celestial hosts
    and the choirs of the whole creation cry,
GLORY be to the Father and to the Son and to the Holy Ghost:
    as it was in the beginning, is now and ever shall be,
               world without end.

That Presence dost thou freely and most wonderfully
            give us;
    first, through him in whose glorious likeness
        we see, O Father, thine,
        thy Son, our Saviour Jesus Christ:
    then, by thine own Spirit
        poured forth without measure from that glory
            upon the sons of thy love,
resting and dwelling in them with all his gifts.

O GOD, thou hast made man in thine own image
        for glory, to live;
        not in the likeness of creatures, to die.
Thou madest us for thyself, hast shewn us thyself,
    lendest thy Presence to light us to thy Presence,
        to joy unspeakable and full of rejoicing.

Father, who ever lovest and wilt not leave us,
    number me among thy sons
        who rest in thy Presence now,
        and lift up their face to thy glory,
           and reflect its light.
Praise the Lord, O my soul: O Lord my GOD, thou art
    exceeding glorious;
GLORY be ....

THE FIRST AND THE LAST

THOU, O GOD, thou art the first,
        thou art the last:
Is there in earth or heaven a God beside thee?
    Beside thee there is NO God,
        nor any goal.

The men of science measure space, measure aeons,
        measure force:
    they cannot measure righteousness,
        nor wisdom, nor love.
No equation, no research, no guess even, can reach
    a majesty so distant and so close.
Thou that art high above all, always,
    dost yet ask room within;
By might of creation, thou art our Father
        but yet more mightily by love.

Eye hath not seen, nor ear heard
    what thou preparest for them who trust on thee.
Even now thou dost bid us come to thee
    that the servant may be where his lord is;
and thou thyself comest to the home of our heart
    that the Lord may be where his servant is.

Thou, O God, art the first and the last,
    our beginning, our end.
As thou dost love and uphold us,
    stir up thy children
        with the sure grasp of faith
            to take hold of thee.

THE ETERNAL

FROM THE LIVING GOD into this world of death
        pours the Eternal.
Seek him; and thou canst not but find it:
    whensoever he comes to us
        he brings the Eternal.

For how can the Eternal Word speak, guide, help,
        but out of the eternal?
    or the Holy Spirit bring his heavenly gifts
        but from the heavenlies?

All that time touches must go.
All that thou givest of thine own, O God,
        has immortal birth and being.
O God the Father, eternal heart of love,
O God the Son, born eternally from the Father's heart,
O Holy Ghost, proceeding eternally
        from the heart of the Father and the Son,
into our hearts thou hast brought thine eternity;
    help us to seek, know, serve, love, inhabit
        the Eternal, now.

If the love of the Eternal be in my heart,
    joy everlasting reigns there.
O heavenly Father, let me be born in thee as thy child!
O Christ, be born in me as my Lord!
O Holy Spirit, with the immortal and infinite
        fill the house of my soul.
O Holy, Blessed, and Glorious Trinity,
    keep, hold me in thy Presence
        eternally.

THE DIVINE LOVE

O LORD GOD, thou art Love,
     Love above all love:
Love that thyself cannot heighten,
    for how mayest thou surpass thyself?
Love that cannot diminish nor decrease,
    for how can Love leave off loving?
Thou art creating wherever love is born;
thou art dwelling wherever love abides;
thou art reigning wherever love rules;
thy warfare, thy long-suffering, all are love;
    love is thy Being and thy Blessedness,
      and thy consuming fire.

The disciple whom Jesus loved bore witness:
Herein is love made perfect,
  he that dwelleth in love dwelleth in God.
His witness we know is true,
    confirmed by all God's saints,
that the love of God makes every labour light,
    —verily thy saints have been heroes of doing:
and that the love of God makes melody in the heart,
    —verily they are earth's apostles of joy:
and that there is no ladder to God but love,
    —have they not shewn us?—
      though it be a ladder of flame.

Lord, bring my sparks and flickers of love
    up to a blaze, and into thy fire;
by love help me identify myself with the love
    that is boundless, endless, divine.

THE MEDIATOR

TWO SIGHTS of truth, O Father of Truth,
    in thy mercy, thy great mercy
        thou wilt not let me see.

The first, thy Majesty;
    the unveiled holiness of thy Being,
    the burning fiery furnace of eternal love;
        too dazzling for human eye,
        too infinite for human thought,
    all worlds beyond, all heavens above
        the horizons of man's soul.

The second, mine own heart,
    ignorant, wilful, mean;
        hugging its little jealousies, loving and loving itself,
its righteousnesses filthy rags
        beside thy holiness, O my God.

Yet by thy mercy, thine own great mercy,
    to bridge between the Glory and the shame,
thou hast ordained and set the Mediator,
    SON OF MAN, SON OF GOD:
Mediator perpetual, mediation complete,
    one offering of a perfect human life,
    one sacrifice of Body, Blood, and Breath;
Priest of our prayer, Bearer of our sin,
    Voice of forgiveness,
        here and in Salem.

BEHOLD THE LAMB OF GOD
    that taketh away the sin of the world—
        and mine.

REDEMPTION

HOLY FATHER, Lord God of Truth,
   as I cannot create myself,
      no more can I redeem myself;
   that power, that gift, is thine only.
Thou who hast made
     alone canst remake.

Remake, redeem me, O my Father!
     What else do I need?
What righteousness have I of myself?
   How can I forgive myself?
   How myself be the propitiation of my sins?
But what we cannot do for ourselves,
   thou hast done for us
      through thy Son our saviour Jesus Christ.

Christ hath taken our flesh upon him,
   faced and felt our tests and sorrows.
Christ hath borne mine own sins in his body
     on the Tree.
Gift, all is gift; boasting is excluded,
   but not gratitude, not joy, not praise.
For all my foolishness and sin, thou dost accept me
      through HIM;
   dost forgive, cleanse, recreate, and renew me
     in HIM.

Complete thy mercy, O Father; to-day and ever
   make me a new creature in Christ.
For the old things are passed away;
     behold, all things are become new,
      through Christ, by thee.

BENEDICTUS DOMINE

BLESSED BE THOU, O Lord, in all things
           that have befallen me:
Blessed be thou in my temptations, when I have continued
        with thee,
    and in thy deliverances when I have wandered away:
Blessed be thou in thy wholesome reproofs,
    in all discipline and chastisement of my pride,
    and in thy lifting up, when I have sought thy face:
Blessed be thou in any advances and victories,
    the whole praise whereof I ascribe unto thee
           with a thankful heart:
Blessed be thou for guiding my steps, most wonderfully,
    when I knew not, understood not, nor even cared:
Blessed be thou for my holy calling,
    for the joy of oblation,
    for communion with thyself,
    for aught thou hast wrought through me:
Blessed be thou for all whom I have loved,
    and who have loved me:
And for THY love, from all eternity, beyond compare
  or compass: merciful, tender, unalterable,
           irremovable.

Blessed be thou in all things that befall me,
    and that shall befall me;
O grant me this last blessing, O GOD of my praise—
    to be true to thee, and close to thee,
         unto the end, without end.

THE WORD OF GOD

BLESSED are they which hear the Word of God and keep it.

LORD, grant me this blessedness
                of thine own promise.
Give me ears to hear, eyes to see,
                and an heart to understand,
        by diligent reading of thy Scriptures,
        in the holy offices of thy Church,
        in private prayer—
to hear, mark, learn, inwardly digest,
                and thoroughly obey:

To hear thy Word, by the kindling of the Holy Ghost,
        in the seeking, reasoning mind,
        in the hungering, thirsting heart,
                in the womb of the soul:

To hear, O Lord, thy Word;
        not the new, but the true;
        not the partial, but the full;
                the final and the eternal:

To hear it, O Lord,
        and with all thy saints and servants
        not only hear, but keep;
        and bring forth fruit
                thirty, sixty, an hundredfold.

GRANT me, O Lord, to take the Book of books
    as from the hands of thine angel,
        with expectancy of faith,
        with brimming hope,
        and with the love that kindles knowledge;
    to open and reopen, read and reread,
        ponder and reponder,
          THY WORD OF LIFE.

Convey to me, O Holy Spirit,
    through the familiar phrases, fresh understanding;
    through passages passed over or unapprehended,
        new treasure;
    through thy grace—insight, conviction, guidance,
        revelation, glory.

Shew me, O Holy Spirit of Light, by the holy Book
    all that has fellowship with light:
    reveal truth, who art Truth,
    illuminate divine mysteries,
    make plain my duties in the eternal order;
        humbling and uplifting the mind,
        waking purpose in the will
          and energy in the deed,
        breathing devotion into the heart,
          exaltation and oblation into the soul:
that I may live and move and rest in thee,
    Father, Son, and Holy Ghost;
        who art GOD alone,
        who art love, who art life,
        who art Spirit, who art a consuming fire
          from everlasting, world without end.

THE GARDENER

O GOD who didst shew thyself in the earliest scripture
    planting a garden eastward in Eden;
We glorify thee
    that thou hast planted a later and a greater in Earth,
        eastward and westward, north and south;
    planned and plotted by thy love, full of divers flowers,
        thy Church of the souls of men.

A garden this, of thy perpetual purpose;
flowers there, of thy sowing, shaping, and cherishing,
    each fair of promise, all different, yet one harmony
        within thy wall and will.
For their springing thou hast set a Star of Bethlehem
        brighter than any sun;
Thou dost water them with the blood of thy love,
    and quicken them by winds of thy Spirit.

What greater delight hast thou than to see earth
        so apparelled, so gemmed?
O sovereign and tender Father,
    keep watch over thy garden and the souls within it.
Guard the root from the slug, the stalk from blight,
    the bud from the worm.
Bring us to full blossom by the openings of faith,
  by purity white as the lily, and by love rich as the rose.
Come near us in thy glory,
    that we may know ourselves planted together in
        Christ's death
    and rising to the likeness of his resurrection.

So, through thy whole garden and all the years,
    shall flowers of innumerable fashionings
    in jubilant multitude of hues,
        reflect thy joy, thy loveliness, THYSELF.

GOODNESS

O MY GOD, thou art good:
    there is none good but thee;
    all greatness thou art, but all goodness first.
My mouth shall speak of thy goodness all the day long,
    for I know no end thereof.

Out of thy goodness thou madest me;
    by thy goodness I know thee;
    for thy goodness I love thee;
    after thy goodness would I walk;
        to the kingdom of thy goodness, come.

It is the fool only that saith, there is no GOD,
        no good one:
thy goodness is immeasurable, unsearchable, unalterable;
    a sea that no land can drain away,
    a land that no sea can swallow,
    a forest that no fire can waste,
    a fire that no water can quench.
What that benefits, what that has made me happy,
    has thy goodness not given?
It follows me all the days of my life,
    and most blessed of all is the promised end
        that we shall see thee, come to thee, live with thee.

Let me begin that heaven here
    through the Spirit thy bounty gives me.
Be the sense of thy goodness ever in my soul
    waking a goodness there to answer thine.
Let the Lord be praised daily
    even the God who shews us his goodness plenteously
        and pours his benefits upon us.
Praise thou the Lord, O my soul!

HONOUR GOD

AS servant and son
    let me seek the honour of GOD and my Father's
        good-pleasure.

In every act
    let me seek the honour of GOD and do his will.
In all knowledge and the search after knowledge
    let me seek the honour of GOD and his truth.
In thought and the train of thought
    let me seek the honour of GOD, his mercifulness,
        his purity.
In planning and purposes, great and small,
    let me seek the honour of GOD and his righteousness.
In all speech and utterance
    let me seek his honour and shew forth his love.
In my prayer
    let me seek his honour and speak his praise.
When I kneel in his house, and before his Altar,
    O my soul, seek the honour and worship of GOD.

Not that GOD has need of my praise;
    it is the joyful due of a servant,
        the love of a son;
    and even so, his own gift.
Therefore waking and sleeping, with all my breath and
        being,
    I shall declare his honour and exalt his Name.

DELIGHT THOU IN THE LORD

O GOD, who callest me son
   despite my sinful leanings
      and promptings to self-pleasure:
Let me, make me, delight in thy law in the inward man,
     not only in high moments, but in all:
   delight in thy purposes, rise up and walk in them;
   delight in thy righteousness and be doing good;
   delight in thy justice and judge accordingly;
   delight in thy forgiveness and humbly give thanks;
   delight in thy love, learn it, dwell in it,
     declare and exhibit it,
        in the power of thy Spirit:
   delight in the inward man,
     and the outward man,
       and the whole man,
     and sing of thy goodness, saying:

Thou, O God, art the thing that I long for;
   and thou, Lord, only, givest us our heart's desire,
   and more than the heart can conceive,
     in thine only-begotten and beloved Son
       our Saviour Jesus Christ.

DEUS DONOR

O THOU that hast given us hands to work:
    Grant us to work faithfully as unto thee
        and not unto men.

THOU that hast given us eyes to see:
    Turn them away from wrongful desire;
        shew them thy handiwork, thy providence,
            thyself.

THOU that hast given us ears to hear:
    Speak in them thy Word; thy Word is truth.

THOU that hast given us minds to think:
    Grant them to consider and contrive that only
        which is pure, lovely, and of good report.

THOU that hast given us tongues to speak:
    Let them tell of thy salvation from day to day,
        and give thanks for a remembrance of thy
            holiness.

THOU that hast given us hearts to love:
    Give us also grace to love thee with all our strength;
        and, for thy sake, our neighbour
        more than ourself.

THOU that hast given us immortal souls:
    Bless us and help us to grow more and more
        into the image of thy glory,
            of thy Son Jesus Christ our Lord.

O LORD MY GOD
  all thine operations around us always,
  all thy gifts and purposes and thoughts,
  all thy redeeming work for all mankind,
    are acts of love.
Grant, O LORD, that thine unimaginable love
  may find in me some love to meet it.
Let me love the love
  that ever loves me.

Thou who by love hast come down to me
    and called me son,
  by thy love wake mine;
wake it to the trust of a son,
  to the obedience of a loving son;
    and lift him up by love to thee.

Deign to unite my love with thine,
  the minute with the mighty,
    the human with the divine;
take whole possession of that thou hast woken,
    purify, widen, and heighten it;
  that my soul's delight may be to love thee
  and what thou lovest,
    and whom thou lovest,
    as thou lovest,
  now and always,
    life without end.

THE DIVINE WORK

O MOST MERCIFUL,
    hear my prayer for grace
    to be a good workman in thy kingdom;
and when thou hearest,
       forgive.

Work in me of thy good pleasure
    both to will and to do thy work,
    the work that thou willest, when thou willest,
      as thou willest;
—thine own incessant work
    of truth, sympathy, healing, joy;
work that speaks, none knows how, nor I,
    the tongue of heaven;
      and reveals thyself.

Thou, O God, art in love with all thy work;
    it flows, it pours, out of thy heart.
In the bounty of thy grace
    make me, O Father, an instrument of it;
the thought be thine, the word thine, the deed thine,
    the glory all thine:
    enough for me
      the obedience.

THY WISDOM, WORKS,
  AND WILL BE DONE

LET GOD PROPOSE;
        not the world, not myself, O Lord,
            but thy providence.
And let GOD dispose:
        not my wilfulness, ignorance, blindness, sin,
            but thy wisdom and thy love.
FIANT CONSILIA TUA:

Yea, let GOD do his work
        with me, for me, in me, through me;
            —the works always of his grace.
FIANT OPERA TUA:

Whatsoever be thy will, O my GOD,
        let it be mine, let me love it,
                for love of thee.
FIAT VOLUNTAS TUA:

O Lord, be ever thy whole will done;
        let me leave all to thy direction
        overcome my reluctances and rebellions;
grant me the confidence of utter trust,
                and its peace.
Lord, of thy deep eternal counsels
        I have no more sight than the blind,
                less knowledge than a child.
        Give me but faith and love—and then

FIANT CONSILIA OPERA VOLUNTAS TUA
NUNC ET SEMPER ET IN SÆCULA SÆCULORUM.

THE GOOD PLEASURE OF GOD
(COLOSSIANS I)

O GOD OUR FATHER
    work upon us and within us thy good pleasure:

Because it hath pleased thee
    through the Son of thy love
        to make us sons of thy love,
    fill us with the knowledge of thy will
        in all spiritual wisdom and understanding;
    make us to bear fruit in every good work:

Because it hath pleased thee
    through the visible body of the Son of man
        to give us an image of the invisible GOD,
    settle us in thy true gospel;
    continue us in this faith, grounded and stedfast:

Because it hath pleased thee
    through the blood of his cross
        to reconcile all things unto thyself;
    strengthen us with all power according to the might
        of thy glory
        unto all endurance and long-suffering with joy:

Because it hath pleased thee
    that he who was from the beginning, before all worlds,
    who created all things,
        should be the first-born from the dead;
    make us to be partakers of the inheritance
        of the saints in light:

Because it hath pleased thee
        to appoint him in all things
                to have the pre-eminence,
        to be head of thy new creation,
                his body, thy Church;
        translate us into the kingdom of the Son of thy love.

Because it hath pleased thee
        that he, in whom all things consist,
                and in whom all fulness dwells,
                should redeem the world,
                should deliver us out of the power of darkness
                and give us the forgiveness of sins;

O, present us holy and without blemish
        and unreprovable before him,
                our LORD JESUS CHRIST;
that in the grace and love of the SPIRIT
        we may give thanks unto thee, O FATHER,
        one GOD, our GOD,
                for ever and ever.

DEUS SACERDOS

O SPIRIT OF GOD, be thou my Priest:
    BAPTIZE me with thy breath
        so that I receive thy life,
            —and my own, eternally.

CONFIRM me with thy fire
    for strength, for probity, for love.

ABSOLVE me from my sins, my many, many sins;

POUR in the OIL and WINE
    to heal my sicknesses by the way:
    cleanse my desires, control my thoughts.

Invite, compel me to the Supper of the King,
    where new born and new clothed
    I may partake of the BODY OF MY LORD,
    and drink the CUP,
        drawn from his wounds.

Nay, close thy hand on mine,
    pledge thou the troth and celebrate the MARRIAGE;
    SPIRIT to spirit,
        Being of GOD to son of man,
            inseparably joined.

ORDAIN me priestly service, O my Priest,
    with spiritual issue of children born to thee,
    and with the altar of thy Cross
        in the deep recesses of my soul.

O Image of the Father, Love of the Son,
    stamp my whole being with thy likeness
    visible by thy grace to others, hidden to me,
        but known when I awake.

VII
THE LORD CHRIST,
GIVER AND GIFT

CHANGE TO THE UNCHANGING

LORD, THOU hast set us amid unresting change.
      Day follows night; season, season; year, year;
           not one the same, nor yet our part in any:
centuries, eras pass, none like the last;
      nature herself is servant to the aeons;
         all things evolve and alter:
change upon change that no man can stay,
      but each must share.

Such thy decree: thou didst accept it for thyself.
      That was the light of God coming into the world.
         a human babe.
      That was the love of God growing in stature
         day after day as we.
      The years of the Eternal drove onward to a cross;
         God's own Son died.

But Christ is risen, is risen!
      and God, for the great love wherewith he loved us,
         has quickened us together with him.
Now One reigns on a timeless throne,
      who changes not.
And God has given us to sit together
      in heavenly places with Christ.
      It is the end of change.
         to abide in HIM.

O death of Christ, the death of death to us!
O life of Christ, now ours, and ours for ever!
Lord, thou wentest our way to become our Way,
      and art our end without an end.
Transform our transient lot, and bring to birth
         within our nature THINE,
      THINE which abides for ever,
         THYSELF in us.

THE LORD CHRIST

I

LET the wisdoms of men clamour and conflict,
        entice, deceive, and pass,
    thy law abideth and guideth;
        THOU, O CHRIST, ART THE WAY;
    no man cometh to the Father but by thee.

Let times and teachings, systems and fashions change,
        thy truth remaineth;
        THOU, O CHRIST, ART THE TRUTH,
    the same yesterday, to-day, and for ever.

Though through the blind night the watchmen still wait
        for the day,
    already the true light shineth;
        THOU, O CHRIST, ART THE LIGHT;
    in whom is no darkness at all.

Though oppressions continue, and hate,
        yet love is stronger than all;
        THOU, O CHRIST, O GOOD SHEPHERD,
          O SAVIOUR, ART LOVE;
    and everyone that loveth is born of God
        and knoweth GOD.

Though death and dissolution seem everywhere to prevail,
        thou hast conquered death, and sin the author of
          death,
    and led captive our captivities;
        THOU, O CHRIST, ART THE RESURRECTION
          AND THE LIFE;
    whoso liveth and believeth in thee shall never die.

Though greed and faction and pride harry mankind
    yet shall not thy children be anxious for to-morrow;
            for Thou, O Christ, art our Peace;
    and thou upon the throne makest all things new.

II

  Yea, O Lord Christ,
in thee hath it been the good pleasure of God
    to sum up all things,
        the things in the heavens and the things upon
            the earth:
and through thee, through the blood of thy Cross,
    to reconcile all things unto himself,
        whether things upon the earth or things in
            the heavens:
that in thy Name, Lord Jesus,
    every knee should bow,
        of things in heaven and things in earth and
            things under the earth:
and that every tongue should confess that thou art Lord,
    to the glory of God the Father.

VENI

COME, LORD JESUS!
Lord, we have looked for thee
      more than watchmen wait for the morning.

Come forth, O Sun, from the eastern chambers:
    though the night be long and dark,
        let the day spring from on high.

Rise, O thou Sun of righteousness
    with healing in thy wings.
Rise, scatter our mean prides and wrong loves,
        the waste of our wraths,
          the gloom of our doubts and failures,
          and all the tyrannies of sin.

Come, Lord Jesus, arise and shine!
Let the whole world wake and kneel
        before the radiance of thy cradle;
    kneel and wonder
        before the bright shining of thy Cross;
    wonder and exult
        in the shattering of thy tomb.

O thou Sun that riseth and never goeth down,
        shine in our heart
to give the light of the knowledge of the glory of God
        in the brightness of thy face;
    and to change us into the same image
        from glory to glory.
Come, Lord Jesus, come!

THE INVITATION

SON of GOD, Son of man, King of kings,
    thou thyself dost invite us:
To thy cradle in Bethlehem
    that we may find thee, meek and lowly of heart:
To thy home in Nazareth,
    that as sons we may grow in our Father's favour:
To the banks of Jordan,
    that confessing our sins we may know our pardon,
        and thy calling:
To the desert of temptation, to continue with thee,
    that our faith may be proved:
To thy places of prayer,
    that thou teach us to pray:
To the company of thy disciples,
    that we may walk with thee and them:
To the mount of Transfiguration,
    that in thy light we may see light:
To the holy Supper,
    that we may dwell in thee and thou in us:
To the garden of Gethsemane,
    that we may watch and choose with thee:
To betrayal, false judgment, and abuse,
    that we fear not to suffer with thee:
To the hill of Calvary,
    bearing our Cross:
To thy holy Sepulchre,
    whence do thou raise us to newness of life:
To the height of the heavens,
    whither thou art gone before:
    and where thou livest and reignest
in the glory of the Father and the Holy Spirit,
    GOD, world without end.

DE SUPERNIS

THOU, O Christ, art from above:
  though thou wouldst dwell in us,
    from above thou comest;
  though thou wilt abide with us,
    in nothing art thou of this world:
the life thou bringest is from above;
the light thou bestowest is from above;
the joy thou kindlest is from heaven;
the peace thou leavest is of heaven.
Every good grace is from thy Spirit,
  every clean and kindly thought,
    every holy longing;
  all my faith, yea, and mine own soul also
    are from thee.
And thou givest thyself, not by measure,
    not upon occasion,
    not in parts and portions,
  but bountifully, tirelessly, illimitably.

O thou that art and comest from above,
  by thy coming give me new heavenly birth,
  new immortal light by thine illumining,
  joy unquenchable by thy healing,
  irremovable peace by thine abiding,
    my Lord and my GOD,
      the same yesterday, to-day, and for ever.

THE LIKENESS

MY GOD, my Father,
    what pleases thee most in us?
    what praises thee best?

Likeness to my Son,
    thy lover, thy Saviour;
Seek, hear, follow him.

O Lord Jesus, draw me toward thine own pattern,
    a son in whom the Father may be well-pleased.
O Holy Child, born upon earth, born into our homes
      to do his will,
    be born in me.
O Saviour, conqueror of pain, sin and death
      by a perfect faith,
    strengthen, fortify, perfect mine.
O Son of man, who shewest us the Father,
      himself in thyself,
    open mine eyes to see.
Son of GOD, light and splendour of the Father's heart.
    flood mine.

O thou who comest to dwell in us,
    yet leavest not the Father's bosom,
    draw my whole soul thither
      as like to like,
    to become more like, and ever more,
      world without end.

MY LORD'S LOVE

I SEE a wonderful kind of love!
   THY HIGHNESS lieth in the straw:
the hands that made the world
     make tiny gestures in a Mother's arms:
the eternal Wisdom, of his own will,
       is powerless to speak, to think.

   Whoso is wise will ponder these things
      and understand the loving kindness of the Lord.

I see a love no less dumbfounding,
   THE KING OF KINGS cursed and cast out:
THY HIGHNESS' head is bowed, thy feet and hands
     fastened with nails, thy blood drops:
the Author of life is done to death
     in the place of skulls,
the Holiest laid with the lowest and worst.

   Whoso is wise will ponder these things
      and know the salvation of God.

I see a glory of love more dazzling yet,
   THY HIGHNESS on the throne of light
     reigning, almighty, eternal;
yet reaching out sleepless hands
     to the weak and sinful children of faith,
  and feeding them on thine own Body and Blood.
This is the Bread which comes down from heaven,
    which only if a man eat shall he not die;
and this the Life given more and more abundantly
     yesterday, to-day, and for ever.

   Whoso is wise will ponder these things
      and adore the Lord of Lords.

THE GREAT PROMISE

LORD, what didst thou mean by that bidding,
    Abide in me and I in you?
by that word, *I am the vine and ye the branches?*
Root and stem, bough, twig, and leaf, the growing tree
    and the flower of fruit, are one—
        one life indivisible, interdependent.
Without thee we can do nothing;
    by thee only bear fruit—much fruit,
        and abide in thy love.

And what mean when thou didst pray
    that thy disciples might be *one with thee,*
    and with thy Father, as thou art one with him?
and that *thou mightest be glorified in us,*
    and *give us thy glory?*
and *that we may be perfected into one?*
    and *be with thee where thou art?*
    and *behold the glory of thy Father?*

Words of wonder passing wonder—
    but thine own, O Truth, O Word of GOD!
Pledge of communion and union with thyself
    passing the bond of friend and friend,
    of parent and child,
    of husband and wife,
        though these are love;
    passing the union of body and soul,
        though these are one;
Closer, closest, is the union of Spirit and spirit
    by thy promise, O Christ, and by thy prayer,
    to the perfecting of peace, of love, of joy,
        world without end.

THE DIVINE PITY

IN THY LOVE and in thy pity
   thou, O Lord Christ, hast redeemed us.
Thine is compassion that knows
    neither limit nor denial.
Sinless thou didst submit thyself to every anguish
   at the hands of sin, at our hands,
    for our sins:
almighty and eternal, thou didst elect to die
   that we might live.

And never will thy pity stale; it burns;
   or fail; it yearns;
    none is forgotten, no, not one.
Nor can any grow into thy likeness
   except he learn pity from thy Spirit,
   except he exercise it in love,
    and shed its peace.

O dearest Lord, whose mercy is over all thy works,
   fulfil my heart's desire:
Set thou this power of pity in my soul,
   guard it and train it there.
From grace of thine make it a ministry of mine,
   to feel the wounds and woes of many;
and, with a wisdom and tenderness from thee,
   to help and heal.

So may both pitied and the pitying discern
   wonder that is, and has been with them all along,
   the pity of our God.

O LORD CHRIST,
    for the world's sake
        thou didst stand against the world;
   thou didst empty thyself,
       that thou mightest fill all things;
   thou wert made a curse,
      to bless all creation.

O Lord, forgive our ignorance, blindness, stupidity;
    our vainglory and cruelty;
    all sin we do in our darkness,
       all our additions to the sufferings of men.

O Lord, let me stand alongside thee
    for cleanness of hand and pureness of heart;
stand after thine example,
    against the small, the shallow, the spiteful and cruel;
stand for the world,
    against the world;
stand for thee and thy righteousnes and love;
    who livest and reignest with the Father and
    the Holy Ghost, God, for ever and ever.

THE TEMPLE

LORD, let me build unto thee a Palace
    wherein my King may dwell,
      that shall be massive and well-wrought without
      and all-glorious within.

Let it have four foundations—
    faith, prayer, good works, and holy learning;
And furniture—nine graces of the Spirit,
    contrition, humility, self-discipline,
    integrity, purity, courage,
      love, joy, peace.

Lord, who hast bidden, *Abide in me and I in you,*
    who dost stand ever at the door and knock,
    let me toil mindfully all day, all ways,
      to build myself for thine indwelling.

Yea, come Lord Jesus, thyself to build;
    for without thee I can do nothing
    nor may the palace be lovely or strong.

Only, O Lord, let it not rise, although thy work,
    a palace, but a TEMPLE;
    the heart of it no throne of state
      but an Altar of Sacrifice,
    whereon in eternal sovereignty is set
      A LAMB AS IT HAD BEEN SLAIN.

ABIDE IN MY LOVE

THOU who didst love us unto the death,
 Lord, thou hast spoken,
  ABIDE YE IN MY LOVE.

Lord, for the great love wherewith thou lovedst us,
  hear the voice of my crying:

my cry from a great way off,
 Lord, I love thee; help thou my lack of love:

the cry of my pilgrimage,
 Lord, I love thee; increase my little love:

the cry of my whole strength,
the prayer of my whole faith,
the whole hope of my heart,
 Lord, I love thee; thou knowest that I love thee;
 make me to love thee more;

Let me find thy love,
  which changes not;
let me know thy love,
  which passes knowledge;
let me abide in thy love,
  who lovest as the Father loves thee,
   in Godhead of love,
    for ever and ever.

ROOM

JESUS, LORD,
>   for whom an inn could find no room,
>   whom thine own world would not receive,
never let me close my door against thee,
>   nor against any the least of thy brethren
>   in their least need.

Stand not then at my door and knock,
>   though that be miracle of mercy;
but lift the latch and enter,
>   Jesus, Lord.

Thou who wast content to die for me,
>   consent to live with me,
>   Jesus, Lord.

Consent, so that there be no place in me
>   from which thou art missing;
>   no corner, but thy light flood it.
Though so narrow my heart
>   let it be all thine,
>   Jesus, Lord.

Enter, perform the whole miracle,
>   Jesus, Lord;
So widen my little room
>   that it holds not only thee,
>   but man, all men,
>   all whom thou holdest in thy heart,
>   Jesus, Lord.

IN CHRIST

CHRIST be in me,
   the hope of glory;
  for joy, for peace,
  for love, for life,
   for death to self.

CHRIST be in me
  to purge my sin
   and heal mine infirmities:
to open mine eyes on the deep things of God
  on new worlds of truth
  and new heavens of love,
   freely given.

CHRIST be in me
  to fight the old man
   and mould the new;
to constrain my thinking, speaking, and doing
  by his Spirit of strength,
  by his Spirit of gentleness;
CHRIST my defence against all mine enemies,
   CHRIST my victory.

O CHRIST, Light of God, light of men,
  dwell in my heart by faith,
  dwell in my mind,
  dwell in my whole being
   to build there thine own image;
until the likeness be nearer like,
  and my life hid with THINE
   IN GOD

REQUIES

HERE we have no continuing city,
    no safe wall of defence,
    no assurance of peace,
    no permission of ease,
    no escape from temptation,
    no relaxing even after repentance.

Yet to the people of GOD remaineth a rest,
    Requies est ipse Christus.
He is our peace, Christ himself, Christ only.

O thou that takest away the sins of the world,
O thou that changest not but abidest for ever,
O thou that dwellest with them of an humble heart,
    grant us thy peace.

O Lord, who, not as the world giveth,
    hast given and givest to us
    this ark and stronghold of peace,
        learn me the true repose;
        —to serve thee without anxiety, without fear,
    with confidence, with cheerfulness, with strength
        and flame,
        all the days of my life.

O LORD CHRIST, who didst offer thyself,
   our Master and GOD,
  to serve thy servants
   to the glory of the Father
   and their own joy and health,
  giving them without measure thine own Spirit:
Help me also to be about my Father's business
   in thy Spirit,
   the Spirit of the Lord:
  and to think every thought
   in the Spirit of the Lord:
  and to speak every word
   in the Spirit of the Lord:
  to discern and confess every fault
   in the Spirit of the Lord:
  to seize all opportunities for good
   in the Spirit of the Lord:
  to do justice without fear
  and mercy without restraint
   in the Spirit of the Lord:
  and to perfect love
   in the Spirit of the Lord.

Yea, Lord, let all my life be worship
   in thy Spirit, by thy Spirit,
    and unto thy Spirit;
who liveth and reigneth with the Father and thee
   in the glory of the one Godhead,
    for ever and ever.

O LORD JESU CHRIST,
 all thy disciples and saints haſt thou driven forth
 into the world to teach the multitudes,
  eaſt and weſt and north and south;
 to teach them by thy faith to believe and live,
    by thy Word to perceive and under-
     ſtand,
    by thy works to love,
    by thy sufferings to prevail;
and in all things always to obey and adore the Father.

O Lord Chriſt, let the whole desire of my heart
 compel me to be such a disciple.
Thou that calleſt the world from the rising up of the sun
 unto the going down of the same,
give me light to learn the grace and truth
 which came by thee,
and power to impart them,
  eaſt and weſt and north and south.

O thou that dwelleſt within me,
 set there thine own will to seek and to save:
 as thou didſt burn with compassion for the multitudes
   who hungered,
  so inflame me;
bid me go forth with the Bread of Life,
  eaſt and weſt and north and south,
by thy might, in thy love, to thy glory:
to whom with the Father and the Holy Spirit, one GOD,
  be dominion and worship, world without end.

ONE THING NEEDFUL

BUT ONE thing is needful,
          not many things:
he that hath the Son hath life:
     he that hath not the Son hath not life.

O God, O Father, thou hast given the children of men
          this one thing, this life,
          freely, fully, wonderfully,
     by giving them thine only-begotten Son.
Grant me, as a child, thy child,
          purity of heart to accept it,
          spiritual understanding to apprehend it,
          a joyful peace in living for it—
life in the same Jesus Christ our Lord.

Let nothing distract me from this one pursuit,
     no unsteadiness of purpose,
     no multiplicity of aims,
     no slavery to special interests,
     no indiscipline of moods,
     no phantasies of desire,
     no faltering of faith,
          no littleness of love.

The one good of life is to give it to thee.
     So Christ be my beginning, Christ my end,
     Christ my way, and Christ my light,
     Christ my energy, and Christ my repose,
     Christ my teacher and Christ my truth,
     Christ my Master and my all-beloved,
          Christ my Life, my Lord, my GOD.

O LORD GOD,
 whose gifts are beyond count or measure or price,
  and every gift, high honour;
of all, this would be chief,
 that thou, O Lord, wouldest write thy Name
  and grave it on my inmost soul
  unknown, unseen, unfelt by me,
  yet readable, for thy sole glory,
   by the eyes of men:
so that it testify in quietness
 to the lowly devotion of my heart,
 the dedication of my whole being,
  the pure joy of faith.

To thy Name, Lord Jesus, help me bow the knee
   and all its worshipping,
  bow the head
   and all its thinking,
  bow the will
   and all its choosing,
  bow the heart
   and all its loving.

But chiefest, O my GOD,
 write thy Name upon me, in me,
 thy holiness, thy lordship, thy love,
  in shining letters,
   indelible, for ever.

VIII

THE DEDICATION

OF LIFE

I BELONG TO GOD

O GOD of heaven and earth, of eternity and time.
>   I BELONG TO THEE,
>   to my Creator, my Father, my Saviour, my LORD.

Though thou dwellest in the light unapproachable,
>   yet come, come according to thine own word,
>   to visit, to take possession of my life.
Though with thee are neither days nor years,
>   yet may I live every minute in thy presence.
Though the ear cannot catch thy voice,
>   thou canst make thy servant hear;
>   speak, Lord, to my soul.
Though the eye cannot detect thy brightness,
>   thou canst touch my faith to sight,
>   and make thyself visible even in my works,
>   and in my pains.
Though thou art Spirit immortal, invulnerable,
>   yet give me sanctuary in thy wounds,
>   and cleansing there.

O Almighty, All-wise, great Father of love,
>   I wholly belong to thee;
do thou in the majesty of thy mercy
>   deign to be mine,
>   my Lord and my GOD,
>   my worship and crown of rejoicing:
in company and alone,
in sickness and in health,
in earth and in heaven,
in time and to eternity
>   world without end.

BIRTH AND BEING

O GOD, thy Gospel hath taught us
      that we are born of thee:
born not of this world, though into this world,
born not of flesh and blood, though into flesh and blood,
born not of the will of the flesh, nor of the will of man,
      though the children of men,
           but of the will of GOD—
born of thy will, of thy love, of thyself,
      O my GOD.

Thou art our Creator, our Father
      breath of our being,
        soul of our soul,
          thou, our eternal Life.
We wear the physical—that is thine;
We incorporate the spiritual—that is thine;
We are not our own, but thine;
      of thy giving only is our freedom,
        our faith, our way, and our goal,
     now and always.

O my GOD, I will give thanks unto thee
      for I am fearfully and wonderfully made.
Thou hast fashioned me, behind and before, without and
        within,
      and laid thine hand upon me;
that my soul knoweth right well,
      and will adore thee for ever.

ONLY THOU, O my GOD, knowest the great eternal
   Purpose—
  of universe, of life, of thy will.
But thy will it is; and thy wielding,
  in process and progress ever;
and that of which we can never see the end or whole,
  nor a corner, nor a day,
may we, by thy will and gift, O GOD,
  learn sufficiently to obey and fit into;
and do thy will in earth as it is in heaven.

Yet, O Christ, thou hast shewn us our part:
  by thy life, by thy words, thyself art the way;
thou givest direction and makest our steps sure;
  thy meat, thy breath was to do the Father's will.
So be my will submitted to his
  joyfully, simply, without looking back or aside.
Let me march the march to GOD,
  let me love where GOD loveth;
with all my sight and might, mind, body, soul, and spirit
  be his will done.

Therefore grant me, Spirit all holy, all wise,
  strength of faith and sight of faith,
  clear enough, strong enough, to fold my life
  into the one eternal sovran Purpose;
and to do the Father's will
  in earth as it is in heaven.

THE VISION

The life of man is the vision of God. IRENAEUS.

GRANT me this life, O Lord GOD,
    this true life, the only true life,
        the vision of thyself.
Draw me to its pursuit
    whatsoever it demand, whithersoever lead.
Bring me to the goal everlasting
        the sight of thy glory,
        the light of thy countenance,
        the heaven of love.

By thy grace, purify my heart and mind,
    increase my faith, confirm my will,
        open the sleeping eyes of my soul.
Make me to see more than I most hope to see,
        far more than I deserve to see,
        more even than I dare to see;
    and, as thou enablest,
        to transmit to others all that I do see.

O GOD, high and lifted up in the temple,
    most holy, holy, holy,
        humble me, cleanse me
        shine upon me and through me;
Vision that art truth, art holiness, art peace,
    that abidest eternally,
        commission and send me;
    so that thou go with me always,
        and I lose thee never.

INTENTION

O Lord God,
    inspire, determine, and enable
                  the INTENTION of my life,
       that it be to thine honour.

Seal it as the desire of my heart,
               the purpose of my mind,
               the goal of my whole strength,
       that it continue single, clear,
                  immutable, importunate.

O Lord,
       be this intention THOU:
          thy truth, thy work, thy love, thy glory.

Let it govern my words,
       burn in all my thoughts,
       purify my dealings,
          occupy and redeem my time.

Let it bring THEE into all my ways
      and the ways of those with whom I have to do;
         —thyself, thy light, thy salvation,
         thy wisdom, thy worship, thy blessing,
            to-day and always.

MY RELIGION, MY LOVE

O LORD GOD, make by religion to be my love,
    my deepest love, my delight, the love of my life.

Let the catholic creed be to me, daily, hourly,
        my hymn of praise,
    as it is also index of my affiance,
        and record of thy bounty,
        and inventory of thy love.

Let me never be content with giving thee
        less than my whole heart;
    and that, with no motive which is not pure
        and no mind which is not joyful.

Make all my days a looking up and a going forth
    to greet and meet that majesty of love
        which hath visited and redeemed thy people:
    —the love that would save to the uttermost
        and is the glory of thy glory,
illimitable, inexhaustible, world without end.

CONSECRATION

O GOD, give me desire,
   overmastering and perpetual,
 to consecrate myself to thee,
      my life to thy Kingdom,
      my love to all whom thou lovest.

Grant me, O my Father,
   not desire only
      but obedience to match,
   and power of oblation,
      through the very Spirit of Jesus.

This day give me grace
      to lift up my soul,
      to pray without ceasing,
      to wait upon thy good pleasure;
 to hear thy voice, speak thy word, do thy will,
      seek thy forgiveness.

And if I have little or nought else to offer,
   accept my faith,
 and keep it unswerving, unafraid, burning
   to welcome thy demands,
      and their cost.

NEW BEGINNING

O LORD GOD, make me die to the old life
    that I may begin the new.
Every good desire, all strong and tender purpose,
    every inspiration to works of love,
        come from thee.
Thou art the beginning of my beginnings,
      well of my fresh springs,
    guide of their channels, guard of their banks,
      goal of their full stream,
      ocean of their rest.

Move me to seek and welcome thy will
    and submit to it willingly and wholly;
for that is the new and the perfect and the endless life,
    every day, every hour.
Thy mercies are new every morning;
      so be my obedience:
    new be my fear of thee
      which is the beginning of wisdom;
    new my prayer,
      school of my faith,
      university of divine learning,
      light of hope;
    and new my love
      which is the crown of these,
      and life eternal.

THE TITLE

I AM THINE by thy desire and operation;
  Thou art mine by thy gift.

LORD, by how many titles am I thine!
  in thee I live and move and have my being;
  my birth is of thy fore-determination,
  my breath of thy breathing, my body of thy fashioning,
  my soul, a spark lighted at thine eternity:
  my home, mine earthly lot, my friends and lovers,
    mine opportunities of good, have been of thy pro-
        viding;
  my tastes, my talents, occupations, calling,
    bestowed by thee for thine employment:

In Baptism, thou didst adopt me for a son;
by Confirmation, hast empowered me for thy work;
in Communion, continuously dost impart thy life.

Lord, what shall I, can I, render back
        for all thou bestowest upon me?
    who am I that thou visitest me?
        and wouldest abide with me?
        and callest me son?
    who, that thou wouldest be made flesh for me,
        be despised and rejected and die for me?

Lord, let me understand better what is above understanding
    and seek to deserve what is ever beyond desert—
I am thine by thy desire, thine operation, thy perpetual love,
    Thou art mine by thine own gift.

ENDOWMENT

O MY GOD,
  what have I that thou hast not given?
 Before thou gavest, it was thine; and thine, after;
   —thy bestowal, thine endowment, of thy nursing
    from child to man, from seed to flower:
  given me to employ to thine honour
  that the son may do the Father's will.

My calling, thy purpose before I was born,
  thine appointment, thy directing through the length
   of days.
All my parts, talents, tastes, duties, opportunities;
  each thy grace, my stewardship;
  in their right exercise, each my gladness and thine;
  my peace in receiving from thee,
    in offering to thee,
    in employing for thee.
Above all, *thine own Spirit,*
    given without measure.

Consecrate thy gifts, O my GOD,
  as thou layest them in my hands
  and breathest them into my mind and soul.
Let me use them, not after my weakness, but in thy strength;
  and glorify thee in all their use.
And do thou by the blessing perfect them
  with the fullest measure that thou wilt,
   unto the likeness of Christ.

LAY HOLD OF THE ETERNAL

GRANT me, O Lord GOD,
     before all things, by day and by night,
     amid all things, imperfect, inconstant, uncertain,
     in small things as in great,
to esteem, to seek after, and to lay hold upon
          THAT WHICH IS ETERNAL.

Truth, in all my conversation,
Generosity, in deed and word and thought,
Integrity and *Sincerity* in all my dealings,
Serenity in anxious and contrary event,
Worth and *Thoroughness* in the occupation both of work
                and leisure,
Patience and *Humility* in my heart,
Thy Holy Spirit in the temple of my soul.

And, by all these, to win
     the freedom and joyfulness
        of a son of GOD
           about his Father's business:
     through Jesus Christ my Lord.

Blessed are they who are installed in the eternal, now:
     theirs is blessedness and eternity ever.

SPIRITUAL TROTH

ALMIGHTY eternal Father,
thou dost marry justice and mercy in thyself,
  God and man in thy Son,
  might and peace in thy Spirit.

O! marry in me
  the fear of thee and the love of thee,
  the knowledge and the practice, of thy will,
  a contrite and a thankful heart,
  the present and the eternal all day long.
Thyself, Lord, be the consort of my soul,
  wedding immortal grace to mortal birth,
  wedding my happiness with thy glory,
  wedding my weakness and thy strength,
   thy desires and my obedience,
   thy Cross and my crown.
O! clothe me with thy wedding garment—
  he that is joined to the Lord
   is one spirit with him.

My Lord and Master, hear me pledge my troth:
  with my body I thee worship,
  with mine understanding, with my heart,
  with all my worldly goods,
  with all thy heavenly gifts,
    I thee worship, thee adore.

Those, Lord, whom thou hast joined together
  let no man, nothing, put asunder.

DEDICATION

POSSESS me, O Lord, my King and my GOD:

Let thy Spirit direct my going out
      and my coming in:
let the promises, the pursuit, the praise of thy glory
      rule the desires of my heart:
let thy light illuminate, thy truth occupy,
      thy wonder fill the chambers of my mind:
let thy love flood all my springs
      of motive and will:
do thou work in and through me as thou wilt please,
      and stifle every whisper of merit or self-seeking:
in the temple of my soul
        be thy Passion the altar,
           thy Presence the priest.

So let me, O Lord, be with thee, and be happy.
May my very life be the vision of thyself,
      my whole being hearken
           to the voice of thy calling,
And every sense and member and breath
      wait upon thy Word
      and run upon thy service,
           my Lord and my GOD.

DIVINE DEMAND

LORD, thou dost offer me all that thou art.
Father, thou dost demand from me all that I am;
    and more, all that I could be in thee,
        that I should be perfect as thou art perfect,
        a son in whom thou art well-pleased,
    a beloved son by whom thou wouldst be glorified.

My Lord, my Father,
    I can but offer thee all that I have been,
    self-stained, self-pleasing, self-glorying, all self;
        and beseech thy cleansing
        and thy Holy Spirit,
    that I may comprehend thy mighty love
        both in gift and demand,
    comprehend, clasp, breathe, absorb it;
    and leaping over the wall of mine own will
        choose thine, and do it.

THE BODY

O MY GOD, I offer to thee my body,
    which thou indeed didst fashion.

Lift it up, as my heart, to thyself:
the good desires of my mind let it translate into deed,
    the bad refuse to obey.
Let my lips be opened
    and as often kept shut, for thine honour.
Let my hands work for thee,
    my feet go about thy business.
Let my knees bend in prayer,
    and my head bow.
Let me laugh with them that laugh
    and weep with them that weep,
        in thy Spirit of love.
Let mine eyes open to see and praise thee everywhere
        in thy visible creation;
        in the sons and daughters thou lovest;
    and close, to worship the King
        immortal, invisible, only wise.

Grant me lordship, full and whole, over my body
    that I may offer it, day by day, to thee
        in a loyal service,
        as a sacrifice, pure and undefiled;
till it become a true temple of thy Spirit,
    ringing with the music of heaven,
    reflecting the likeness of Jesus,
        now and always.

DOMINE QUID VIS FACERE?

FATHER, *what wilt thou have me to do?*

MY SON, take no thought for the morrow;
    be perfect TO-DAY.
Give unto me the present,
    this minute, this moment;
  let to-morrow look after itself;
    eternity is now for all life lived in me.
Be good and true of heart now;
    labour for peace now;
    speak the word of love now;
    pray without ceasing in a quiet heart.
Do my will in tranquillity,
    without hesitation,
    with all thy might.
Treat all thy work, day by day, as mine;
    for mine it is,
    and my Spirit thine.
And I, who have begun it in thee,
    will finish and perfect it
      unto the end,
        without end.

LORD, *make me content to do thy will:*
  let thy law live and burn within my heart
    now, always.

RETURN UNTO THE LORD THY GOD

O LORD, who alone teachest men knowledge,
    lead me back to the ONE BEGINNING
        that I may learn thy Truth.

After I have journeyed through the years, through the
        months,
    (not less, at the end of each single day,)
        let me return unto the ONE BEGINNING.
After I have read many books,
    and sought wisdom by study;
after much experience of joy
    and some of sorrow;
after long search for beauty,
    unsatisfied by the outward eye;
after exercising what authority has been entrusted to me,
    after performing the humble duties to hand;
in all perplexity of mind, vexation of heart, weariness
        of spirit,
    after failure and sin—
make me return to the ONE BEGINNING,
    that I may begin again.

Yea, after I have loved the Faith,
        and the place where thine honour dwelleth,
        and thy Scriptures and Sacraments,
        and have watched in prayer,
    bring me back always to the ONE BEGINNING,
        to THYSELF,
    my Father, my Saviour, my Life, my Glory,
        world without end.

NON NOBIS DOMINE

O MY LORD and GOD,
      what have I that I have not received?

Let me not attribute unto myself
      what is from thee, and thy sole gift:
      my breath, sustenance, bodily senses, and health;
      my home, parents, pastors, masters, friends, and
                 benefactors;
      all whom thou hast given me to love;
      my studies, recreations and pursuits;
      the talents and pounds of thine entrusting;
      my vocation and the callings within it;
         my happiness;

Let me not attribute to myself
      any seeming success or station of influence,
      any virtue, or delight in the excellent,
      not my faith, nor works, nor readiness to pray,
         love of thy will, search after thy likeness;

All these, if or so far as they be, are from thee;
      less than thou wouldest give or hadst given
      could I have more faithfully received,
         more humbly and gratefully recognised
         thy hand.

If I glory at all, let me glory in THEE,
      ascribe the praise where only it belongs,
         unto thee,
      and thy mindful, unceasing, illimitable love,
         my Lord and my GOD.

INTERCESSION

Inspire me, O Lord God, after the example of Christ,
    to love my neighbour,
  not as myself, but more than myself;
and where outward help is out of human reach
    to have a true, lively, inward sympathy,
    a pity and continuous prayer
             for the needs and agonies of men:

For children with wretched homes or none at all;
    the agéd, the maimed, the halt, the blind, the
                  tormented, the mad;
    voyagers, holiday-makers, workers in dangerous
                  places,
  weak souls struggling through the day,
  sick souls crying through the night,
         the sinful in great cities and dark haunts.
And when before thee, O God, I look on these
    let me see beside them, in them, Christ crucified.

Let the less than neighbours become more than brothers;
    let me love by prayer, help me pray them into strength,
           into thy mercies, into newness of life:
  tens of hundreds whose names I cannot know,
  the thousands who know not thee:
  —let all be guests in my heart
    and loved in thee,
who lovest all, who lovest each, who art love,
        omniscient, omnipotent, eternal.

THE EYE OF THE SOUL

LORD, open thou mine eyes!
The outward sight, the eyes of my body,
    thou hast given me in full measure,
        for which I praise and bless thee.
In the visible scene I joy and rejoice,
and, in the fitness and loveliness of creation,
        acclaim and learn the Creator.

But open more and more, O Lord, the eyes of my mind
    to read and understand thy salvation
    and to trace the blessed, endless life of the Saviour,
        in the lives of the faithful,
          in the lineament of saints.

Above all give me faith, the eye of the soul,
to know thee and Jesus Christ whom thou hast sent;
    know thee in thyself and for thyself
        uncreate, incarnate, omnipresent;
    all goodness, all compassion, all purity, all fire,
        Father, Son, and Holy Ghost,
          dwelling in the light inaccessible.

Lord, that I may receive this inward sight
    which thou alone canst implant,
        thou alone illumine,
          thou alone fulfil,
a faith that never sleeps
        and eyes that never close!

THE TREASURE

LORD, thou hast given me so much to love
     here, now, upon earth,
things most lovely, and lives yet dearer:
hast given not only my love for them,
     but theirs for me.
O let me see, grasp, cherish, thy gifts!
     and not be blind or oblivious,
     nor lose nor spoil nor shame them.

The apprehension of all this love
     brings further gifts from thee:
deep senses of purification, of thy purposes in time,
of grace governing and upholding all,
of a secret glory behind the outward scene,
     and of thine own love, immortal, immutable,
        freely given.

So from the many things I love here,
     all given by thee,
let me draw a wealth that cannot waste,
     brought to my small quays
        by the galleons of heaven;
and know that thou, who givest love,
     ART love;
and he who dwells in love
     dwells in thee.

INQUIETUM EST COR MEUM
DONEC REQUIESCAT IN TE

Let me rest in God alone,
    my light and my salvation,
    my health and my glory,
    the help of my countenance and my hiding-place,
    the rock of my whole strength,
        my God for ever and ever.
Inquietum est cor meum Domine donec requiescat in te.

The resting-place of souls is nowhere else than heaven,
    nowhere but in union with our Father;
    there they belong, even now.
Let me learn to rest even now in God alone,
    as I ought,
    as I would,
    as God would;
    above all goods and gifts,
        all fame and praise,
        all other loves,
        all doubts, despondencies, and sorrows.
Inquietum est cor meum Domine donec requiescat in te.

Let me rest, O God, in thee alone
    for there is none like unto thee,
    all good, all wise, all loving,
    most wonderful in thy holy places,
    the brightness of immortal glory,
    the eternal rest of saints.
Inquietum est cor meum Domine donec requiescat in te.

IX

THE GIFTS OF GRACE

LET GRACE REIGN

LET GRACE reign!
    thy grace, O Father, O Son, O Holy Spirit.
Thou, O Lord, art the Sovereign Lover of souls,
    only by thy grace can we be saved,
        saved through faith.

What a Kingdom is this; of thy grace,
    dispensing the eternal and the kind
        bountifully, boundlessly!
Grant us, with songs of thanksgiving,
    to desire and take its exceeding riches
        as our most royal heritage,
        as the highest wonder of thy power,
            as all hope fulfilled and surpassed.

This is truth ſtablished in the heavens,
    this the noble law of thy kingdom—
that thy mercy is set up for ever,
        so that we come behind in no gift,
    receiving grace upon grace:
and not leaſt, grace to love as we are loved,
    with all our faith, obedience, and strength,
        with all our heart and mind and soul.

Let us then come boldly to the throne of grace
    to find help in time of need,
        to learn thy love and thy salvation.
Let thy grace reign, O Lord,
    everywhere and for all,
        through righteousness unto eternal life.
Nay, by a yet more royal bounty,
    incorporate us, O King of kings,
        into thy very mercifulness, into thyself;
        and raise us to thy Throne.

THE SOURCE OF GRACE

All things are to be sought in God alone,
every good and perfect gift, coming down from heaven
   in the hands of the Son of his love;

Forgiveness, brought us by his WORD;
Wisdom, (not of this world, but of God), in him crucified;
Light, for he is light; and Truth, for he is truth;
Love beyond love—who made me, and my home on earth,
   who seeketh me out when I wander from the way,
   who suffered and died for me and all mankind;
his Calling, which is without repentance;
his Spirit, which he giveth not by measure;
Rest, for he only is our peace;
Joy, if we attend upon his will;
Blessedness, if we abide in him;
Life, more abundant and eternal, in himself, the Life;
   —All things are to be sought in God alone
     through Jesus Christ our Lord.

And all things are to be received from GOD,
   and used and occupied for GOD,
   to bear fruit through GOD.
O my soul, wait thou still upon GOD,
   who filleth all things living with plenteousness;
to whom be the praise, the power, and the glory,
     for ever and ever. Amen.

I

O MY GOD,
 from this world of darkness, sham, and shame
let me look in faith up to the light of thy grace;
  work, learn, love,
    by the light of thy grace;
  live and die
    in the light of thy grace;
  come to mount Sion,
    through the light of thy grace;
  and with an innumerable company of angels,
  with the spirits of just men made perfect,
    exult in thy light and thy grace;
O my Lord and my GOD,
    both now and for ever.

II

O LORD, lift up the light of thy countenance upon us,
    that in thy light we may see light;
  the light of self-knowledge
    whereby we may repent;
  the light of faith
    whereby to choose thy will;
  the light of guidance
    whereby we may advance;
  the light of grace
    whereby we may attain;
  the light of glory
    which shineth more and more unto the
      perfect day,
    and unto thyself, the very Light of Light;
  who livest and reignest in the brightness of
    the holy and undivided Trinity,
    blessed for ever and ever.

ONCE AND FOR EVER
    thou didst plunge me, O Lord God,
not into a little font,
    but into a boundless ocean
        of a Father's love:
and thence didst draw me forth,
        cleansed and glistering,
    new born, new clothed
        with Spirit and Light.

Out of captivity, out of the Egypt of sin,
    thou hast brought me forth into the Promised Land;
    to a new home in the sinless Body
        of thine only-begotten Son.
In him thou didst give me sonship
        eternal and divine,
    and a priesthood, royal and indelible,
        sealed with his Cross.

Thou, O God, callest all thy children by name;
    in thy Book of life
        write mine among them.
Abba, Father; confirm me in Christ's grace,
    hold me in his Body,
    build me into his likeness
        by thy most holy Spirit, evermore.

THE FINGER OF GOD is come upon us
      by his Holy Spirit.
We who are learning the love of a Father, know it;
we who have seen Jesus, know it;
we upon whom the Holy Spirit has fallen
      know it:
      the finger of God has come upon us.

Be thou the breath of our breath, O Holy Spirit,
      the thought of our thought, the light of our light,
        the love of our love.
Bring thy health to our infirmity,
      thy vigour to our health,
        thy generosity to our vigour.
Let us walk in the Spirit and repose in the Spirit,
      work with the Spirit, judge after the Spirit;
by the Spirit let us make melody in our hearts
      unto the Spirit, always.

If thou dwell in us, O Holy Spirit,
      we dwell in heaven;
      we are passed from death unto life;
All is light, new light; and love, new love;
      and power, new power;
      and fountains of joy,
      by thy gift, by thy Presence.

Verily, the finger of God is come upon us.
O Holy Spirit, heal us, hold us, lead us,
      fill and fulfil us,
      always, ever.

THE BEST GIFTS

O LORD JESUS CHRIST,
    who givest holy things
        by thine own holy sacrifice,
        by thine own holy sacrament,
        by thine own Holy Spirit,
    without measure and beyond understanding:

Incline and inspire us
    to covet earnestly the best gifts,
    to pray for them fervently,
    to work for them diligently,
        for faith, for hope, for love,
        for humility, and self-control,
        for truthfulness and right judgment,
        for every foundation of peace;

And to receive them, nothing doubting,
    with the song of thanksgiving,
    and the offering of a whole heart unto thee;
who livest and reignest in the glory of the eternal Trinity,
        God, world without end.

THE LORD'S MERCIES

LORD CHRIST, we praise thee for thy mercies:
  the mercies that are new every morning;
  the help on which all day we depend;
  the divine privilege and intercourse of prayer;
  the love encompassing us on every side;
    thy persevering mercies to me,
      a wilful son,
      a wilful sinner.

Be thou praised for the mercies of thy Church and grace,
  pledged and performed by thy sacraments:
  my clothing with thy sonship
    in holy Baptism;
  mine arming with thy Holy Spirit
    in Confirmation;
  my pardoning through the blood of the Cross
    in Penance;
  the imparting of thine own heavenly life
    in Holy Communion;
    —all this to me, a wilful son,
      a wilful sinner.

Praise the Lord, O my soul,
  for the mercy of that calling to ministry,
    of which thou repentest not,
      despite my wilfulness;
  for the mercy of thine inseparable Presence,
    despite my sin;
  for the mercy of a boundless, endless hope
    and the promise of everlasting life,
      sealed by thy blood.

My song shall be always of the loving kindness
      of the Lord;
  praise the Lord, O my soul,
      evermore and evermore.

DETACHMENT

BESTOW upon thy servant, O Lord,
        the grace of detachment;
the will and power to withdraw from the importunities
          alike of the world and self;
        from allurements that engross and are waste,
          and the oppression of passing cares.

Teach me to look beyond the world,
        and to set every day
          into the frame of the heavenly vision,
Bid me to enter Jerusalem which is above,
        mine inheritance by water and the spirit
          in the land of the living.
By prayer and sacred study open a door in heaven,
        where I may converse with the blessed,
          sing in David's choir,
          bathe in the river of life,
          pluck the leaves of healing,
          kneel in the light of the Lamb.

There, in thy Spirit and Presence,
        let me speak with my soul;
      in the Holy of Holies,
        adore without words.
There as in my native country
        let me take hold of eternity,
      and bring it back to serve thy will
        in the small details of time.

ILLUMINATION

LIGHTEN mine eyes, O most holy Lord,
    that they be not blind to the wondrous things of
        thy law;
        more wondrous, of thy goodness;
          most wondrous, of thy love.

Unstop mine ears, that they fail not to hear
        the ceaseless music of thy mercies,
        the harmonies of thy truth,
          thine own still small voice.

Penetrate my mind, that all the day long
        it may search out the deep things of thy Spirit,
        in thy light see light,
          and be stayed on thee.

Irradiate my heart, that it love only
        what is true, what is just,
        what is pure, lovely, and of good report;
        and through all that it loves,
          love thee.

Dazzle my soul, that, while I have any being,
        I may sing praises unto my GOD,
        and dwell in thy house all the days of my life,
          even for ever and ever.

FAITH

GRANT ME FAITH, O Lord God;
    more than acknowledgment of thy being,
    more than a deep veneration for Jesus of Nazareth,
    more than an honest repetition of Creeds,
    more than convinced assent to Catholic doctrine;
But a faith like Christ's faith
    undiscourageable, invincible, glowing, and complete.

A faith in my Father,
    who made me and all the world,
    who loves me and has redeemed me by his own Son;
a faith in my Saviour,
    who loved me more than his own life
    and imparts to me his own Spirit;
a faith in the Holy Spirit,
    breath of faith, giver of faith, life of faith;

a faith creative and abounding in good works,
    not in word but in prayer,
    indefatigable, indomitable, moving mountains;
yet in penitence and dependence
    praying, praising, enduring to the end;
faith all from thee, in thee, and unto thee,
    Father, Son, and Holy Spirit,
        my Lord and my GOD.

FAITH

O LORD GOD, increase my faith,
        so that it rule for life my heart, mind, and soul:
By faith let me confess Jesus Christ Lord and God
           with my mouth and whole being;
        confess Jesus incarnate and Jesus crucified,
        and that thou hast raised him from the dead.
By faith let me apprehend my Father, Redeemer, Life-giver;
        Deity, Divinity, Unity, Trinity:
           make me to live by faith.

By faith may I perceive that which is invisible,
        the good as good, truth as true, the kingdom
                       of Spirit
      and the powers of the eternal world.
By faith let me hold to thee, who first hast holden me,
        and wilt not let me go:
      set me by faith on the immovable rock
      of thy strength and peace.
By faith impel me to the works of thy will,
        to present to thee all the energies of my being
      and answer love by love.
By faith let me face with joy any trial of my faith,
        and never refuse to partake of Christ's
                   sufferings:
      lead me to win by faith the victories of faith,
      and overcome the world.

By faith grant me even now the company of the faithful
        who have pleased thee in all generations,
      and reflect for ever thy light.
By faith bring me to the rest that remaineth for thine own,
      and to Jesus, the author and finisher of faith.
By faith let me humbly and thankfully receive
        the wonder of thy blessing,
     O Father, Son, and Holy Ghost,
        to-day, to-morrow, evermore.

TRUTH

SET TRUTH within me, O Lord GOD:
stablish and settle the love of it in heart and mind,
    exalt and enthrone it in my inmost soul.

So that I may be grounded and built upon its integrity,
        illumined by its light,
        and girded with its honour:

so that I may trust its counsels,
        walk in its ways,
        and obey its demands to the end:

so that I may repose upon its strength,
        stand unafraid in adversity,
        burn for its propagation,
        and battle that it may prevail.

O grant, when grace has led me to thee,
        that truth may hold me there;
—truth that is eternal,
        righteous, divine,
truth that is THOU,
        my Lord and my GOD.

OBEDIENCE

THOU, O crucified Master, for the joy that was set
                                        before thee,
    didst learn and shew us a perfect obedience
        by the things which thou didst suffer.

In our little needs and sorrows,
        in misfortune and pain,
    keep us, O Lord, from complaint;
    keep us, above all, from self-pity;
    give thine own joy and valour
        to help take up our cross and follow.

All thine apostles were martyrs;
    no cosy religion, no half obedience, theirs.
They obeyed God rather than man;
    they endured as seeing him who is invisible;
    they wandered without home over the wide world,
        yet never left thee;
    they suffered hardness, indignity, the shedding
                                        of blood,
        Lord Jesus, with thee;
    and gave thanks.

Make us, like them, unafraid of our cross;
    nay, bless it, and by thy mercy unite it
        to the saving power of thine.
Thou, who hast brought so many sons to glory
        BY THY CROSS,
    grant us to praise thee with a song,
        as we take up our own.

LOVE

God is love. ST JOHN

We please God when we are most like him. TRAHERNE

MULTIPLY LOVE in us, O Father of love,
    that we may please thee well,
        serve thee best,
        glorify thee most;
            who hast first loved us.

Multiply love in us, O loving Saviour,
    that we may work the works of love,
        call forth in others the lovable and good,
        bind up wounded spirits
            and ensue peace;
    after thy pattern, who hast first loved us,

Multiply love in us, O Holy Spirit,
    who workest in love through the history of man,
        that love may cast out fear, despondency,
            pride, and all little or evil thinkings,
    that we may bring forth the full fruit of love
            in gladness of heart
            and in readiness to suffer;
    that thou mayest accomplish in us
            thy purpose of love
    who didst first love us.

Multiply love in us, O Holy, Blessed, and Glorious Trinity,
        who hast first loved us,
        who art love,
    that, best and most, we may love THYSELF;
    by love adore thee,
    by love learn thee,
        and by love wake up after thy likeness,
            our GOD and our All.

TRUE LOVE

O LORD CHRIST, thou haſt shewn and we have seen
    that True Love leads to all good,
    and toils for the perfecting of kindness;
that True Love burns behind all thinking and perception,
    rejoices with them that do rejoice,
        and weeps with them that weep.
True love always longs for thee,
    and draws from thee,
    and dwells in thee;
        for thou art Love.

True love brings the very image of THYSELF,
        into our soul's heart.
It is the movement of thy Spirit in our wills;
    thy tone, thy temper, in our speaking,
    thine outlook, thine insight, in our seeing,
    thy hand in our doing and our refraining to do,
    thy sword in our battle,
    thy joy and blessing within us,
        to-day, always.

Be eager and humble, O my soul,
        to learn this love,
which clothes our being with thy beauty here,
        and with immortality hereafter.
O Lord, transform my unloving impulses
        into thine own tenderness,
    that I may learn to love as thou loveſt,
        and as I am loved.

HUMILITY

O CHRIST, my Lord, sovereign Lord of heaven and earth,
    thou, humbling thyself to dwell among men,
        didst choose always the place
           which would arouse no envy,
           which no pride would approach or inhabit;
    a poor maid's womb for making thee babe;
    a cattle-stall for thy cradle;
    saw, hammer, and chisel for thy schooling;
    nowhere to lay thine head,
        though thou wert teaching the whole world;
    spitting for thy face, the lash for thy back,
        thorns for crown;
    bare wood, sharp iron for thy bed of death;
        for thy Godhead, a grave in earth.

Humility has no pattern but thee.

By thy lowliness, O Lord,
    slay my worst foe in me,
    slay thy worst foe in me,
        my pride, and all its little satisfactions,
           and its cravings for more.
And enable me, for thy glory,
    to imitate thy glory,
        and heart, mind and soul,
           to choose the lowest room.

HUMILITY

O MASTER and Lord,
    thou that art meek and lowly of heart,
    thou that hast told us to learn of thee,
        teach me to be little in my own eyes;
        bestow the grace of humility
  which thou didst so wonderfully grace;
            as corner-stone to every virtue,
            as doom and death to pride,
            as rest unto my soul.

Bestow it, through the avenue of holy fear,
        for that thou art very high exalted,
           all sovereign, all holy,
        the first, the last, the everliving One,
and I, apart from thee, nothing.

Bestow it, better, through a lively gratitude
    to thee, who hast given me being by thy Word
        and sonship by the Cross;
        who hast guarded, guided, and forgiven me,
        called and recalled me
to thy work, thy suffering, thy victory, thy peace.

But, most and best, of thy love
    bestow a lowliness flaming with love,
        that asks nothing but to give,
        claims nothing but to serve,
        and offers heart, mind, soul, and strength
to THEE WHO GIVEST ALL
        and, above all, THYSELF.

DEPENDENCE

LET me depend on GOD alone:
      who never changes,
      who knows what is best for me
         so much better than I;
    and gives in a thousand ways, at all times,
      all that the perfect Father can
         for the son's good growth—
      things needful, things salutary,
      things wise, beneficent, and happy.

Thy gifts and will are one:
      it is thy being to will and give what is best:
for thy will issues from thy love;
      the more I do thy will, the more I learn thy love;
and the more I learn thy love, the more am I impelled
        to do thy whole will.
So, Father, thy will be sought, be found,
      be followed, loved, and finished.

Thou art a Father who sayest,
   ALL THAT I HAVE IS THINE.
Let me give thee all that, by thy Holy Spirit, I can be.
Let me think only of pleasing thee,
    holding nothing back, neither complaining nor
         refusing;
    but depending joyfully on thee
      for thine inspiration, to do well;
      for thy power, to do better;
      for thy love, to carry love among men;
    for thine overshadowing in the passing hour of
        trouble
      and in the infinite day of peace.

SIMPLICITY

GRANT me, O my God, the grace of simplicity;
    singleness and candour of heart,
    tranquil certainty of faith,
    joyous sincerity in intercourse,
    good-will and trust towards all;
        white garments, these, of the children of Christ.

Make me so to repose on thee
    that I be not disturbed by the demands and surprises
           of to-day
      nor by the threats of to-morrow;
    nor study the conduct or intrigues of others,
    nor serve at all the standards of the world.
Let me not ask to comprehend thy motions and measures;
    but pursue them, when thou shewest them,
        without question and with joy.

Quietly may I love,
    quietly obey, quietly pray;
quietly and honestly bear my witness,
    generously think and speak,
      never seeking to impress or be clever.
Thou, O Father, hast set a little Child in our midst:
    make me a child in soul,
      a child in purity,
    a child like that Holy Child,
      more, more, and ever more.

PEACE

GRANT me, O GOD, the great gift of thy peace,
    throughout the day and in the night season:
using in quietness all the faculties thou hast given.
Bestow a tranquillity of mind and soul
      out of a faith settled and lively,
      secure from the world's fevers,
      serene in the knowledge of thy nearness,
          and of thy perfect, unchanging will;
      dwelling in the light eternal
          and the truth invisible,
    drawing from the wells of thy wisdom.

In the world we may have tribulation;
    in thee we shall have peace.

But let this peace be never a flight or escape
      from issues of difficulty,
      from right decision,
      from open war against wrong;
never passive, but aglow with Christ's Spirit,
          and Christ's love.

This abundance of peace grant me, O Lord GOD,
    so long as the moon endureth:
and, as thou givest what is beyond understanding,
      help me to receive lowly and worshipfully
         what is beyond gratitude:
      through the same thy Son Christ Jesus,
        Prince of our peace,
           now and for ever.

TRANQUILLITY

LORD JESUS, by thine own peace of soul,
    rooted and living in the eternal Father,
    serene in the hours of commotion and anguish,
        grant me thy tranquillity.
Be my life hid in thine;
    let thy fearless and imperturbable Spirit
        come to dwell in mine.

Thou hast said, *I will give you rest:*
    thy presence is our peace.
Thy Spirit is the donor of every good grace,
    and, in all that he bestows, brings with him
    thine eternal purpose, thy divine counsel,
    thy support and most ready help,
    thy courage and thy victory,
        thy love.
Whom then, what then, shall I fear?

Whom then, what then, shall I fear?
    Thou who guidest us in the calm
      wilt not leave us in the storm.

So let me be still; and inwardly worship,
    in private, in public, everywhere, always,
    and know that thou art GOD,
        my GOD, GOD with me.
Be thou the rock of my repose,
    the moving pillar before and behind my pilgrimage;
    not as the world gives
        giving thy peace.

GRACE OF SPEECH AND SILENCE

OF THY GRACE, O Lord,
    set a watch before my mouth
    and keep the door of my lips.
Restrain me, save me
    from all dominance, or display in conversation,
    from self-congratulation, open or disguised,
    from self-pleasing in play of words or wit,
        and all exaggeration for effect;
    from gossip, complaining, and self-pity,
    from spite, hate, and the will to wound,
    from discourtesy, harshness, cynicism, and contempt,
    from worldly talk and laughter out of season.
For I am utterly purposed that my mouth shall not offend.

Rather, Lord, lead me to establish
    the disciplines of kindly speech,
        and sympathy of listening;
    the spirit of holy silence
        inwardly recollecting thee;
    and the joy of making melody in my heart
        with hymns and psalms and spiritual songs.

Yet open thou, O Lord, my lips in thy praises
    and still more my soul, to magnify thee in quiet,
        by faith uplifted to the heavens,
        by love rejoicing in my Saviour;
        NON CLAMOR SED AMOR
            PSALLIT IN AURE DEI.

CONTROL OF THOUGHT

Pensée fait le grandeur de l'homme
Toute la dignité de l'homme consist en la pensée.   PASCAL.

MAN'S GREATNESS lies in his power of thought,
    in this consists all his dignity:
        without, he would be but a brute or a stone:
    and this is the kingdom
        which God gives each servant to rule.
O GOD, the giver of my sovereignty,
    who searchest me out and knowest me
    and understandest my thoughts long before,
        help me to think as I ought;
    to control and hallow my thoughts
        as incessantly as they are born, tarry, and pass.
O my GOD, keep incorrupt and generous their sequences
        and imaginations,
    their courtesies, reasonings, and critical judgments;
lift them up to thy holy places
    that their measure be always the true and the eternal,
        discerning new wonders of thy love and will,
        rejoicing in the glory that is beyond thought.
O guard my kingdom from sudden surprise,
    from prolonged or recurring assault
        by world, flesh, or devil;
    and from the constant importunate tyranny of self.
And because we become what we love,
    whatsoever things are true, whatsoever honest,
        whatsoever just, whatsoever pure,
        whatsoever lovely, whatsoever of good report,
    if there be any virtue, and if there be any praise,
        O Lord, let me think on these things.
Prove, O Lord, and examine, purify, and still my thoughts,
        and keep them in the glad prison of thine
           obedience.

GRACE BY PAIN

HAVE I no wounds to offer to my Saviour;
    who gave me Five of his, and full fifty times five?
to which I've added by the pricks and blows of my self-will
    other five hundreds, above all count.

Pain cannot but visit, on its occasions, this body of mine,
    and with thrusts as fierce the mind, the heart,
        the soul;
pains wholly *mine*; but they become pure grace of thy giving
    if offered up in prayer and shouldered to thy praise;
—scratches and troubles of an hour, no doubt, no more,
    yet stigmata, little stigmata, if brought to thee,
    the marks of the Lord Jesus on my being,
    wee supplements to one divine immeasurable pain,
    our mortal gift to an immortal love;
        and thus made healing for thy hand to use.

O shew us plain the beauty of that compassion
        for human misery and loss and guilt
    which drove thy body and heart to suffer so!
Teach us the fortitude of One
    who turned the waste of suffering into gain,
    and tortured, forsaken, dying, and alone,
        redeemed a world.

Such stigmata as we can receive from thee and lift to thee,
    let thy grace send.
Make clear both when and how I must take up the cross
    and follow thy wounded feet:
    for to enter the Passion of my Lord and GOD
    is highest Grace of all.

JOY

THE BEAUTY of the earth,
    the radiance of saints,
    the clean strength of truth,
the whole wonder and world of good will
        proceed from the joy of God.

May the joy that is thine, O my God,
        become also mine;
let it shine through me, gleaming with faith,
    beaming with hope, teeming with love,
        unquenchable in pain.

Tune the strings of my spirit
        to the music of thine:
make me bring to the company of the faithful,
        —nay, of all men—
a humble, repentant, lively, singing gladness:
    let me meet and defeat the devil, all devils,
        with a smile.

Dear God, what, in the whole universe, is this Joy?
    No less, none other than the Lord Jesus Christ.
He that hath the Son, hath life,
    thy life and the music and marvels of it.
Christ is the author of all joyfulnesses
        that are pure and enduring;
Christ, their communicator
        every day and all day long:
Christ, their end
        beyond mortal horizons.
All joy is mine, to all eternity;
    for I am Christ's,
        and Christ is God's.

HAPPINESS

LET THY GOOD PLEASURE, O my GOD,
  be my whole happiness;
 and pleasing thee, my supreme good.
Let me learn, and love to learn, that true joy,
  which none can know outside of thee;
for happiness is thy will, O GOD,
   happiness perfect, eternal, in THEE.

First, by the confession of a contrite heart,
  grant me the joyful liberty of the forgiven.
Bow unto thyself the knees of a grateful son,
  take the cheerful surrender of my soul.
Let thy Holy Spirit fill full all the room that is in it,
  with hope, love, confidence, and peace.
Let me live for all that hath thee and thine for an end
  and begin, continue, and complete all to thy glory.
Be THOU the crown of my rejoicing;
  and mine, the ceaseless hymn of heaven—

BLESSING AND GLORY AND WISDOM AND THANKSGIVING
 AND HONOUR AND POWER AND MIGHT
  BE UNTO OUR GOD FOR EVER AND EVER. AMEN.

X

THE LATTER DAYS

OLD AGE

O LORD GOD, who leavest us not
    nor forsakest in the time of age;
Shew me, as my strength faileth,
      an even fuller lovelier light of thy glory
          shining over and about me.
    O my soul, give thanks!

There in that glory, let me find mine.
Grant me new store of gentleness, gratitude, patience;
      new learning of the Passion of my Lord;
         new dignity of Grace.
Make my life wholly his life: his heart, my heart;
    his breath, my breath, breathing love
        to the very end.
    O my soul, give thanks!

My time is in thy hand
    Be thou my support in weakness,
        my courage in the dark and in pain,
        mine aid, day and night,
        my company in loneliness,
        my rest.
    O my soul, give thanks!

For all that thou takest from me,
    thou givest what is better,
      and guidest to the best.
    O my soul, give thanks!

Be thy love my bed and covering,
    be thy Christ my living Bread;
      thy Spirit, my strength to the end.
Bring me forth, forgiven, loved, and loving,
    son and servant for ever,
      into thy joy.
    O my soul, give thanks!

MY JUDGE

MY GOD, when thou bringest me to Judgment,
  grant me, the guilty, this last grace—
   to cite myself against myself;
telling the truth without excuse
   to the very corners of conscience.
Then judge not, O Lord, according to my desert,
   but forgive: forgive and cleanse.

O my God, I am ashamed before thee
  for what I have been
   and for what I am;
and no less ashamed,
  for what I am not,
   but with thy ready help could have become.
Let me lament before thee
  all of thy giving which I have spoiled or wasted,
   not heeded, or refused to use:
O remember not the sins and offences of my youth,
   nor of mine age:
  be merciful to my sin, for it is great.

My Judge, my Father, forgive and cleanse,
   for Jesus' sake.
Yet spare not this:
  sentence me to the clear, the whole, the bitter sight
   of my ingratitude and sin—
  against the vision of THYSELF,
   thy purity, thy cross, thy love.

PRAY IN PEACE.
    Thy God is so near:
    thy God by his own choosing resides within thee.
Does he not want to speak, to hear?
        has he not asked the intercourse of trust,
            the give and take of love?

Pray in peace;
        lifting thine eyes to look upon thy Lord;
            to look intently,
as once, O Saviour, another malefactor looked,
            and took thy hand to heaven.

Pray in peace;
        the peace of nearness to the Holy;
        a peace of contrite awe,
            trembling, but with joy;
        for it has all,
            O Christ, in thee.

Never wilt thou turn thyself, Lord, from my prayer,
        nor me from thy Presence.
O Lord, keep me as close to thee
        as thou art, by thy grace, to me.
Then in thy peace
            I shall know mine.

PRAYER IN WEAKNESS

SPIRIT OF GOD, how close thou art!
   —closer than air or light or breath.
Thou dost envelop, invade, occupy, govern,
   but never weigh down nor crush.
How can the holy Spirit of Love weigh down?
   Or the Spirit of Joy crush?
How the Spirit of Peace oppress,
      how thyself?

Spirit of God, how close thou art!
   past word, past worship, wonderful;
      music of joy,
      clasp that is peace,
      kiss of flame!

Yet at thy touch and closer than touch,
   let thy fire of mercy
      burn up my sin,
consume my old sins and my new,
   my ingratitude, oblivions, and perversities,
      by thy Presence.

Then in thine own time, O Holy Spirit, O Comforter,
   bear me, shriven and contrite,
      to God's heart, home.

THE COUNTRY

God is the country of the soul. ST AUGUSTINE

NO LONGER is the country of God far off;
    faith is nearing sight,
        and the long search, possession.
Yet even there we shall continue seeking,
        so wonderful, so inexhaustible it is;
—A country beyond storm or change,
    where rest is complete, but always awake,
        active upon a Father's miracles of good;
    where light illumines love, and love dazzles light,
        where righteousness and peace kiss each other;
    where there are no more shames,
        and no more tears.

Thou art thyself, O God, that country,
        art Eden everlasting;
    thyself the tree of healing for mankind,
    thyself the river of our cleansing,
    thyself the slaking of our thirst,
        thyself full truth and perfect knowledge
GOD HIMSELF, the country of my soul;
    thou my beginning before I was born,
        my end without an end.

God bring me to this country!
    God help me by the hand,
    God clothe me with his grace,
    God fold me in his life,
        for evermore.

JUBILA DEO

LET ME SING unto the Lord,
 sing praises joyfully unto the Most High:
sing to the Lord of all the earth,
sing to the Lord of the whole heavens,
 sing a new song unto the Lord my God.

Never will I cease to sing praises
   unto my God:
sing with words and without words,
sing in the daytime and in the dark,
sing with my understanding and with my heart,
 rehearse with my whole being my song,
All my fresh springs shall be in thee, O Lord.

—Rehearse it with the choirs of heaven
   and with their joy.
From the eternal let it ring
 through the transiencies of every day.
To the eternal let it leap,
 from thee and to thee, O my God!

THOU, O Father almighty, thou art my song;
THOU, O Son my Saviour, thou its theme;
THOU, O Spirit of Love, its stream and melody.
O Holy, Blessed, and Glorious Trinity,
 lift my praises to the heavenly choirs
  even now; and always.

THE LAST SURRENDER

LORD OF ALL LIFE, the Eternal,
 thou art a God
  who didst embrace death.

Yet from the tomb on earth,
 where men laid thy body,
thou didst disclose LIFE,
  life without end.

There in that sepulchre, buried deep and dead,
 lies for ever the dread of death.
THOU LIVEST: thou givest glory of life,
  LIFE WITH THEE.

Lord, as my mortal hours run by,
 help me to die to the flesh, die to myself,
 die to all that is not of thy Spirit,
  die daily.
So that I make the last surrender of this life,
 not to death, but to GOD.

Give my soul hunger for its remaking
  by its Beloved, in light:
and bring me to the finishing of faith,
 to my own Easter day,
  IN THEE.

THE MUSIC OF HEAVEN

IN LIFE ETERNAL the redeemed sing thy praises,
   Lord God Almighty,
ten thousand times ten thousand
   in the orchestra of heaven,
    Alleluia, Alleluia:
and all first touched and practised on this earth
   their instruments of music,
faith, generosity and joy, integrity, patience, courage,
    Alleluia, Alleluia.

There, in the communion of saints,
   the lamentation for sin,
   the dirges of pain and sorrow,
    are left behind.
There, creed has become paean;
   and all the sympathies and sacrifices of earth
    build into one hymn,
    Alleluia, Alleluia.

O make my life, O Lord, to its very end
   rehearse melodies for heaven!
Let truth sing in my soul
   and love frame new descants,
    be they never so simple, so faint,
   to the eternal chorus,
    Alleluia, Alleluia, Alleluia.

MOTHER
1864 – August 12, 1951

THIS IS HER BIRTHDAY, once born into this world,
   HER BIRTHDAY, born again into life eternal.
O Christ, give her safe passage!
O Christ, give her sweet greeting!
Be thyself her birthday gift
    surpassing all others ever—
       thine absolution to cleanse her,
       thy kiss to welcome,
       thy light to clothe.

Let her best-beloved comfort her,
      loved on earth and now met again:
Let her rejoice with choirs of angels
    and companies of the redeemed
in the streets of the City,
      in green pastures.

She lieth in white
      with the smile of a bride;
She lieth still—
      surely, O Christ, thy peace is hers—
    and very lovely,
      surely, in thine, her loveliness is new fashioned.
She lieth as one praying,
      undoubtful, content,
      who hath found and seen.

By thy Cross and Passion
    which, wonderfully, world without end,
      doth plead for our salvation,
    deliver her, O Jesu,
      from all pains of death,
      from all pains of new birth,
      from all wounds of sin
      and memories of sorrow.
By thy Resurrection and Ascension
    be her life, her Joy, her Day,
      for ever and ever.

SOURCES

These prayers the preface calls a mosaic. To disentangle origins, whether of suggestion or phrase, of quotation or echo, is now beyond my own powers and knowledge. The Latin in 177, for instance, I found, in undergraduate days, written round the choir stalls of the apse of S. Damiano, Assisi. Gerard's Herball started 105. The sources range from these unusual places to the Bible, which appears in almost every prayer.

Liturgy appears in the Antiphon on which 46 rests. 137 starts from a phrase of St Irenaeus; 129 of St Chrysostom; 95, 135, and 186 of St Augustine; more than I can remember (e.g. 86) from the wisdom of the Imitatio; one (121) from Ludovico Vives, translated in Christian Prayers 1578; 178 from Pascal; 169 from Traherne. Eckhart with his profound flashes of insight announced the themes of 71, 120, and 142. Echoes, full or faint, from St Mechtilde of Magdeburg (66, 170), Tauler, Henry Vaughan (11, 28), and Caussade are there too, somewhere! Jeremy Taylor's Sermons are audible in 2, 12, 23, 31, 35, and 94. Still more influential is Donne; 36 and 106 turn the core of his Sermons VIII and XIV (Alford Ed.) into prayer; the Confession at 27 derives from Sermon CVII, though Donne himself was quoting it from a 16th c. source which I once stumbled across and since have been unable to trace. His mastery of expression influences at least 75 and 145; I suspect others also; for Donne has an unparalleled power of kindling the vision which turns into prayer. Among moderns the like inspiration proceeds from Fr Congreve S.S.J.E: 37 and 148 are of his kindling (Spiritual Progress, Sermon VII, Christian Life XX); 21 and 176 owe him phrases.

The two brief prayers at 63 are reprints from Daily Prayer, by kind permission of the Oxford University Press; 82 and 90 appeared first in A Procession of Passion Prayers (S.P.C.K.). 28 has been used as a General Confession on several National Occasions (National Day of Prayer 1947, Festival of Britain 1951, Remembrance Sunday, throughout).